THE WALTER LYNWOOD FLEMING
LECTURES IN SOUTHERN HISTORY

LOUISIANA STATE UNIVERSITY

Lincoln and the South

J. G. RANDALL
Professor of History, University of Illinois

GREENWOOD PRESS, PUBLISHERS
WESTPORT, CONNECTICUT

Library of Congress Cataloging in Publication Data

Randall, James Garfield, 1881-1953.
  Lincoln and the South.

     Reprint of the ed. published by Louisiana State
University Press, Baton Rouge, in series: The
Walter Lynwood Fleming lectures in Southern
history.
     1. Lincoln, Abraham, Pres. U.S., 1809-1865--Ad-
dresses, essays, lectures. 2. Southern States--
Politics and government--1775-1865--Addresses,
essays, lectures. 3. Presidents--United States--
Biography--Addresses, essays, lectures. I. Title.
II. Series: Walter Lynwood Fleming lectures in
Southern history.
  E457.8.R1818   1980   973.7ꞌ092ꞌ4 [B]   80-22084
  ISBN 0-313-22843-4 (lib. bdg.)

Reprinted in 1980 by Greenwood Press,
a division of Congressional Information Service, Inc.
88 Post Road West, Westport, Connecticut 06881

Printed in the United States of America

10 9 8 7 6 5 4 3 2 1

To the Beloved Rebel
who abides with me

AUTHOR'S PREFACE

In preparing these lectures for publication there has been some final revision, and passages which were shortened or omitted in delivery have been kept intact. In the main, however, the lectures are presented here as orally given. The visit to Baton Rouge was a delightful interlude; the author and his wife cannot adequately express their grateful appreciation of the many courtesies extended by the University. The cordiality of this Southern welcome, the gracious hospitality of students, faculty, and community, will be long remembered.

This is a small book on a very large subject. Certain aspects of the theme are not even touched; for those that are presented the treatment has necessarily been greatly condensed. Within the dimensions of four lectures it has been possible only to suggest main trends; the occasion and the purpose have allowed no opportunity for elaboration, much less for documentation. Fuller discussion of some (though not all) of these matters appears in a two-volume work by the author which was in press while the lectures were presented— *Lincoln the President: Springfield to Gettysburg.*

Scholars have long been aware of the distinguished work promoted by Louisiana State University in the field of Southern history. By its Press, its periodicals, its notable manuscript collection, and its productive faculty this work has in recent years been amply sustained and intensified. For the kindness of Professor Walter Prichard and President W. B. Hatcher, and the valuable co-operation of Professor Marcus M. Wilkerson, the author desires to make special acknowledgment.

J. G. RANDALL

University of Illinois
Urbana, Illinois
August 31, 1945

CONTENTS

ILLUSTRATIONS

I

WHEN LINCOLN LOOKED SOUTH

It IS appropriate to begin this lecture with a
quotation from Walter Lynwood Fleming. Of
Abraham Lincoln he said: "Better than most
Union leaders he appreciated conditions in the
South . . . and the advantage of calling in the
old Southern leaders. He was generous and con-
siderate. . . ." (*The Sequel of Appommattox,*
63–64.) This statement was applied to the President whose sense of unhappy duty involved the use
of force against Southern armies. Nevertheless,
leading Southern writers, and many Southerners
of that troubled time, have agreed with Fleming.
With this statement as a kind of text, it is the
purpose of these lectures to look into Lincoln's
background, his prewar attitude, his presidential
dealing, and his postwar outlook with a view to
their bearing upon Southern relations.

[1]

Lincoln was of the North, but it should not be forgotten that he was bound to the South by ties that were fundamental and experiences that were emotionally underlined. He was referred to as a Southerner by some and even by himself. In 1864 a Northern delegation conferred with him concerning escaped slaves coming within Union lines. It was urged by this delegation that their pay as laborers should be comparable to that of whites. The purpose of the interview is not our main point, nor is it very pertinent to note that one of the delegation described the President as being "seated at his desk with his long legs on the top of it, his hands on his head and looking exactly like a huge katydid or grass-hopper." As for the description, it might be tagged and labeled as one of the less known of Lincoln's portraits drawn from life, but some of Lincoln's quoted remarks on this occasion come well in hand for our present purpose.

After hearing the arguments the President is said to have remarked "with one of those peculiar smiles of his, 'Well, gentlemen, you wish the pay of "Cuffie" raised.' " A young member of the delegation—one Henry Samuel, aged twenty-five —said to the President: "Excuse me, Mr. Lincoln,

the term 'Cuffie' is not in our vernacular . . . ,"
adding that their purpose was to have "the wages
of the American Colored Laborer . . . equalized
with those of the American White Laborer." To
this the President is said to have responded: "I
stand corrected, young man, but you know I am by
birth a Southerner and in our section that term is
applied without any idea of an offensive nature. I
will, however, at the earliest possible moment do
all in my power to accede to your request."

The word "Cuffy" applied to a Negro slave was
a familiar bit of Southern colloquialism in the
antebellum period. Lincoln used the Southern
vernacular; he knew shades of meaning that to a
Northerner—at least to many Northerners—
were a closed book. He spoke and understood the
Southern language.

One of the journalists of the day wrote as
follows: "Western and Northern-bred men ought
not to forget that Lincoln was of the South." The
author of this statement was an exuberant news-
paperman who today would be called a columnist
—perhaps a Drew Pearson of his time. His name
was George Alfred Townsend and he wrote under
the name of "Gath." The quoted passage is in O.
H. Oldroyd, *The Lincoln Memorial: Album Im-*

[3]

mortelles (p. 513). As a journalist giving a statement that would have general significance, Gath was thinking of Lincoln in a representative capacity. In elaborating his thought he referred to "honest Southernhood taken into Northernhood."

Another case in point is recorded as occurring in the days of the crisis over Fort Sumter. Two justices of the Supreme Court—Nelson of New York and Campbell of Alabama—were conferring with Seward. The Secretary of State, feeling that he could not quite accede to their suggestions, which in his opinion would have involved recognition of the Confederate government, said: "I wish I could do it. See Montgomery Blair, see Mr. Bates, see Mr. Lincoln himself; I wish you would: they are all Southern men."

Here are three cases where Lincoln was referred to as a Southerner: by a contemporary journalist, by his Secretary of State, and by himself. Did Southerners so regard him? For the most part in his own day the obvious answer is in the negative, but it is curious to notice the bracketing of his name along with that of Jefferson Davis when Kentuckians got around to the selection of two men to represent that proud state in Statuary Hall in the Capitol at Washington.

The two men actually chosen for Kentucky were Henry Clay because of his outstanding political distinction and Ephraim McDowell because of his contribution to medical science and perhaps also because he was not a politician. School children and teachers of Kentucky, while the matter was in process of being decided, were asked to express their preferences, and in the somewhat unimpressive returns no one had a majority; but the curious fact is that "Lincoln had the most votes, followed by Daniel Boone and Clay," according to Frank L. McVey, president of the University of Kentucky and chairman of the Kentucky commission appointed to make the selection. (The statement was made by President McVey in a letter to the author, May 12, 1944.) Many of those who favored Lincoln also favored Jefferson Davis as a kind of running mate.

The idea that the two historic leaders of opposing governments—Lincoln and Davis—should have been seriously proposed by some Kentuckians as the two men out of all their history to represent their state is a believe-it-or-not item which ought

[5]

perhaps to be dismissed as a curiosity or added to the collection of the well-known Mr. Ripley. The purpose is not to exaggerate its significance here. The distinction of Clay among Kentucky's political leaders was outstanding. The commission felt that Lincoln was a national or a world figure whose political life belonged to Illinois while that of Davis belonged to Mississippi; they wisely judged that Kentucky did not need to go that far afield.

The relation, however, of Lincoln to Kentucky —which, as no one will deny, is a Southern state— is a solid and substantial fact. Kentucky had sentimental memories for him. He did not himself remember the farm of the Sinking Spring near Hodgen's mill where he was born; but he did have vivid memories of that other Kentucky home to which the Lincolns moved when Abraham was two years old—"on Knob Creek, on the road from Bardstown, Kentucky, to Nashville, Tennessee, at a point three or three and a half miles south or southwest of Atherton's Ferry, on the Rolling Fork." This region of early Kentucky was Abraham Lincoln's little world in boyhood years. The adventures and wonders, the primitive labors of a growing lad were associated with this creekside cabin home. This "Knobby" and "Knotty" locality, as Dennis Hanks called it, was indelibly impressed on Lincoln's memory. Dependent on the spring for water that had to be laboriously carried, and upon a distant mill for grinding the family grist, the Lincolns lived close to nature; fish and game supplied much of their food. The family was poor; the woods and the creek about them were givers of life itself. It was here that Lincoln had his earliest primitive schooling. It was natural that when he thought of Kentucky he did not think merely of something on the map; he thought of his parents, of Muldraugh's Hill, of Knob Creek, of the Rolling Fork, of boyhood escapades, of hunting and fishing, of dropping seeds into the ground—things that were elemental.

Lincoln was born in the South. His parents, lowly though they were, had one supreme distinction—they were both born in Virginia! What more could one ask? The pattern of the Lincoln migrations—those of the Lincoln family down the decades—was a part of the historic stream of settlement that included George Rogers Clark and other notable Southerners who helped to build the West. The background was English and in the earlier generations the American background was Massachusetts and Pennsylvania, but as the generations moved closer to Lincoln the ancestral setting was the Old Dominion.

If it meant something to have an ancestor in the Plymouth colony, Lincoln could claim that honor, though he cared little for such tombstone distinction. As for Virginia ancestry, perhaps the combination of a Virginia great-grandfather, a Virginia grandfather and a Virginia-born father would serve fairly well, and Lincoln had all of those if he cared to use them. "Virginia John" Lincoln was his great-grandfather; Abraham Lincoln of Virginia and Kentucky was his grandfather; Thomas Lincoln, born in Virginia, was his father.

Lincoln himself wrote in his autobiography in 1860: "The grandfather, Abraham, had four brothers—Isaac, Jacob, John, and Thomas. So far as known, the descendants of Jacob and John are still in Virginia. Isaac went to a place near where Virginia, North Carolina, and Tennessee join; and his descendants are in that region." He then went on to speak of the three sons and two daughters of his grandfather Lincoln. He mentioned Thomas, his father, Mordecai, who "remained in Kentucky till late in life," and Josiah, who removed to Indiana; then he added: "The eldest sister, Mary, married Ralph Crume, and some of her descendants are now known to be in Breckenridge [sic] County, Kentucky. The second sister, Nancy, married William Brumfield, and her family are not known to have left Kentucky. . . ." This mention of uncles and aunts is given here not for its own sake but because such details are typical of good old Kentucky pioneer families. Had the Lincoln clan been assembled in the year 1860, though they did not go by clans or think in those terms, the majority of them would have come from Southern homes and the place of rendezvous might well have been in Kentucky.

Ties to Kentucky held strong and sure. One never fully throws off the feeling he has for the state of his birth. So it was with Lincoln. His speech in mature life has been identified as the Kentucky idiom. His partner, William H. Herndon (in a letter to Theodore Parker, August 23, 1858) referred to him as "a Kentucky gentleman." In the bitter days to come he was to be called a "Kentucky mule," but at least the Kentucky connection was not forgotten.

When dealing with the Lincoln theme one finds it hard to remain always on the level of solemn academic discourse, especially if treating the pioneer period, and there now comes to mind a homely incident of the days when the Lincolns were establishing themselves in Indiana after leaving Kentucky. Dennis Hanks told how Thomas Lincoln drove "his stalk Hoggs" and left them at Posey's near the Ohio on the Indiana side. How he got them across the river is not stated. Dennis Hanks and another Kentucky relative, Thomas Sparrow, who had accompanied the elder Lincoln and the hogs, had returned home; but within a week, said Dennis, "here cum all the Hoggs A Bare had got in a Mung them Killed one this was a Bout 80 miles the[y] Cum." Those pigs lacked the pioneer spirit. Whatever may have been their prospect of life, liberty, and the pursuit of happiness on the Indiana side, or of helping to build American civilization in the wilderness, they could not resist the Southern call of their old Kentucky home.

On two occasions Lincoln made speeches in Cincinnati—in September 1859 and February 1861—and in each case he addressed part of his remarks in the friendliest spirit to fellow citizens of Kentucky. In the 1859 speech he suggested that there might be Kentuckians in his audience and remarked: ". . . by speaking distinctly I should not wonder if some of the Kentuckians would hear me on the other side of the river." In February 1861 at Cincinnati he mentioned that he had previously "addressed much of what I had said to the Kentuckians" and added: "Fellow-citizens of Kentucky!—friends!—brethren! may I call you in my new position? I see no occasion, and feel no inclination, to retract a word of this. If it shall not be made good, be assured the fault shall not be mine."

But Lincoln left Kentucky at the age of seven and never after that was his home in a Southern state. What of those later years, which were nearly his whole life? The answer is that as a boy and growing youth in the woods of southern Indiana, as a young man in New Salem, Illinois, and as a mature man in the fuller years, Lincoln was still immersed in Southern influences. The dispersion of Southern human types, mores, and thought patterns, throughout the West and Northwest was a notable thing; Lincoln was precisely a part of that transit of culture by which Southern characteristics took hold in Northern states.

One does not by any means exhaust the subject of Southernism when he speaks only of strictly Southern commonwealths. Even today, when one moves about in southern Indiana—the delight of artists and genre writers—he cannot but realize that he is in the midst of cultural influences that derive from the South. If that is true today, it was incontestably true in the years 1816 to 1830 when Lincoln was growing up "like the forest oak" (as Herndon said) in Indiana. After Lincoln's death, when Herndon was collecting material in southern Indiana touching the far-off days of Lincoln's early life, he talked with one Mrs. Crawford, who had lived near the Lincolns. The interview was recorded in Herndon's indefatigable style, and on the manuscript he wrote: "Mrs Crawford is a lady of the Ky stamp." He could have said the same of many of Lincoln's Indiana neighbors.

The Hoosier state in those aspects that were close to the South was part of Lincoln. Even in the matter of slavery early Indiana showed the qualities of a Southern community. In the congressional session of 1805–1806 a petition came from the people of the then territory of Indiana asking Congress to permit slavery in that territory despite the solemn prohibition of the institution in the Northwest Ordinance of 1787. They believed that legalization of slavery would promote settlement and that it would even benefit the Negroes, whose masters would have fewer slaves with more room to look after them and less motive to sell them South. The request was not granted, but this friendliness to slavery in early Indiana is to be noted as part of our recollection that the people of that territory and commonwealth in the earlier years were essentially Southerners.

It was so also in Illinois, which kept many of the characteristics of a slave state at least as late as 1840, and which, from Springfield south to picturesque Shawneetown and Cairo, presented in marked degree those human aspects, cultural types, and mannerisms that characterized Dixie.

Mention of Shawneetown and Cairo brings to mind the Ohio and the Mississippi. Those broad rivers were part of Lincoln. They seized powerfully upon his imagination as a youth. We need not speculate as to how far he was fired with the ambition to become a steamboat man, as in the case of Sam Clemens, but we know that the fascination of river life held its spell over him and that much of his serious thought was given to problems of river navigation. He mentioned this subject in his early political utterances; he was chosen to assist in piloting the *Talisman* on the proud occasion when it puffed its way up the Sangamon and had to be

steered amid shallows, snags, and overhanging
branches to avoid disaster. His interest in river
navigation also led him to become the inventor of a
device for lifting river steamboats over shoals.

It is obvious that this river interest had its
Southern aspects. Lincoln's trips by flatboat to
New Orleans—first from a point on the Ohio in
southern Indiana when he was nineteen, and later
in 1831 when he made the trip with one companion
from Old Sangamon Town on the Sangamon River
—were the occasions of Lincoln's earliest contacts
with the deep South. Drifting down the powerful
spring current gave him sights, adventures, thrills,
and mishaps which he did not forget. It was thus
that Lincoln first saw Louisiana, and in the busy
harbor of the Crescent City he saw tall-masted
ocean ships side by side with paddle-wheeled river
boats and those pioneer rafts built of hewn timbers
cut for the purpose and discarded after the one
downward voyage. Unfortunately we have no
record of his passing Baton Rouge, or of the
manner in which as a lad he observed the cosmo-
politan culture of old New Orleans with its court-
yards and balconies, but we know that he had never
entered a larger city up to that time. It was there
that he first looked through broad windows into

the larger world beyond Pigeon Creek. Having visited New Orleans in 1831 as a terminus of his "boat enterprise," as he called it, he settled at New Salem; but Southern scenes beyond the bend of the Sangamon were occasionally in his thoughts. For that matter he had no need to go beyond the bend to mingle with Southerners; he needed only to look about him.

Dwellers in that briefly flourishing hamlet on the Sangamon—indeed, the inhabitants of old Menard County, Illinois—had an unmistakably Southern background. James Rutledge and John Cameron, founders and city fathers of New Salem, are good examples of former Southerners who had migrated to Illinois. Rutledge was born in South Carolina; the family had come up through Georgia and Tennessee to Kentucky. Cameron was a native of Georgia. One could go down the roster and note that the same was true of many others in New Salem and in the surrounding country. If there were any who spoke with the Yankee twang, they were conspicuous by their peculiarity. It was the same when Lincoln went as a member of the Illinois legislature to the early capital at Vandalia. It was so at Springfield, where men from Virginia, Kentucky, and Tennessee were numerous among

the pioneers of Sangamon County. Nor was it different when he moved about on the famous eighth
judicial circuit of central Illinois counties, where
his associates included men of Southern birth, such
as Orville H. Browning and Ward Hill Lamon.
All three of Lincoln's Springfield law partners
—John Todd Stuart, Stephen T. Logan, and
William H. Herndon—were born in Kentucky.
In the case of Stuart and Logan, their back-
grounds, eminently typical of pioneer Kentucky,
were on the more favored social level. A Scotch-
Irish Presbyterian, Stuart was born near Lexington, son of a Transylvania University professor,
and was educated at Centre College, Danville,
Kentucky. The grandfather whom he had in common with Mary Todd Lincoln, General Levi
Todd, was a distinguished leader who took his
part in the battle of Blue Licks, and whose estate,
"Ellerslie," was in the very heart of the Blue
Grass, not far from Henry Clay's "Ashland."
Stephen T. Logan's ancestry was Scotch-Irish and
partly English; in his case as in Stuart's much of
the early chronicles of Kentucky could be read in
the personal stories of his family. Logan was educated in Kentucky and lingered there long enough
to practice law before coming to Sangamon

County, Illinois. William H. Herndon was a mere infant when he left Kentucky, but he came of an old Virginia family which reached back to the seventeenth century and was prominently connected with other well-placed families of the Old Dominion. His ardent antislavery zeal set him apart from others of his background, proving a source of offense to his father; but Herndon always referred to himself as a Southerner—e. g., in writing to Theodore Parker—and expressed himself eloquently in appreciation of Southern elements among Western pioneers.

Though Abraham Lincoln is often thought of as a backwoods character, partly because of overemphasis on his sobriquet of "railsplitter," yet when he was only thirty-four years old and not yet widely prominent, he was actually regarded as "the candidate of pride, wealth, and aristocratic family distinction." This, he wrote to a friend, "would astonish, if not amuse, the older citizens" who had known him as a "friendless, uneducated, penniless boy, working on a flatboat at ten dollars per month." "Yet," he added, "so . . . it was."

This more favored family connection brings us to the subject of Lincoln's marriage to a Southerner and what it meant in his life and achievement. Here we approach a tangled problem and an injustice. Public opinion has usually regarded Mary Todd Lincoln as a termagant and shrew, and set in contrast to a scolding, sharp-tongued wife the lovely, romantic figure of young Ann Rutledge of New Salem. This popular conception has taken away from Lincoln's faithful wife for more than twenty-two years the love her husband gave her, and bestowed it upon the vague image of this girl whom he knew in his youth. The chief promoter of this impression, both in the overemphasis on Ann Rutledge and the unkindness toward Mrs. Lincoln, was William H. Herndon, Lincoln's exuberant partner and biographer.

Herndon is a fascinating study. A roughhewn man of the frontier with an amazing intellectual activity, he was steeped in New England transcendentalism; to this he added a passion for reading minds and explaining things by amateur psychoanalysis. He conceived of his life of Lincoln as a study in psychology, not a narrative. He professed reverence for the truth and sought it laboriously; he had also a genius for distorting it by the workings of a mind that was itself in need of psychoanalysis. Yet he considered himself clairvoyant in discernment; had he been of the opposite sex his processes could have been attributed to woman's intuition. In justice it should be added that Herndon's record does have value when critically used. In collecting letters and records from other people and preserving them, he rendered a service for which historians are grateful; the Herndon-Weik manuscripts are a rich and vast collection. Since it is only recently that they have become generally available to historical scholars, we are only beginning to get an adequate appraisal of Herndon's interpretation. The availability of this collection has now made possible an examination and evaluation of his material.

It was Mary Todd Lincoln's misfortune that this crude, vigorous, and mentally slanted individual set her picture before the world. It was not in Herndon's cultural horizon to understand the vivacious, high-bred daughter of an aristocratic Southern family, or her tastes and standards; nor could he estimate the value of these things to her husband. He could comprehend best her faults and weaknesses, her fits of temper and lack of self-control, and the little incidents of these failings that became backdoor gossip in Springfield. Out of these incidents (indirectly transmitted), out of an acquaintanceship kept distant by mutual dislike and disapproval, and out of a vast deal of his own psychoanalysis, he presented Mary Lincoln as a vicious woman who married her husband to make him miserable and succeeded thoroughly. And when after Lincoln's death Herndon collected reminiscences of a beautiful girl named Ann Rutledge who had died in 1835 in New Salem, and whose death was said to have plunged Lincoln in grief despite her engagement to another man, he built up, perhaps in compensation, a romance that rested upon thirty-year-old memory and tradition, too vague and contradictory to be the stuff of fully authenticated history.

After a troubled courtship Lincoln and Mary Todd were married in 1842. This courtship involved a broken engagement which emerged from Herndon's fluent pen as a wedding at which the bridegroom did not appear. There was no defaulting bridegroom. An examination of evidence gives basis only for an emotional crisis and severed engagement which cast Lincoln into deep gloom, the essence of which was his fear that he had made Mary Todd unhappy. Despite these disturbances the struggling young lawyer was fascinated by the popular belle, a vivacious leader of the cream of

MRS. LINCOLN

Some thirteen years before this picture was taken, Lincoln had written in one of his playful and affectionate letters to his wife: "I am afraid you will get so well, and fat, and young, as to be wanting to marry again."

Springfield society who lived in the handsome mansion of her sister, Mrs. Ninian Edwards.

Mary Todd's early background included the richness and beauty of life found in a prominent family of the Old South: stately home in Lexington, Kentucky (now fallen into decay and degradation), fine family carriage with liveried coachman, beloved house servants, beautiful clothes, extensive hospitality, picturesque and spacious living. The Todds were a proud Kentucky family and there was reason for their pride even if there is point to the tradition of Lincoln's once saying that, while one *d* was enough to spell God, it took two *d*'s for Todd! Lincoln felt the lack of advantages in his early life, and what Mary Todd brought him in her social training, her early acquaintance with the prominent figures of Lexington, her absorbing interest in politics and its workings, was of real value to her husband. It was one of their congenialities that they loved intensely this game of politics and both were ambitious for Lincoln's political advancement. Common interests bound them together; each supplied qualities which the other lacked. Where he was abstracted and melancholy, she was animated and cheerful; where he was concerned with justice and prosperity for the people, she was concerned with justice and prosperity for Mary Lincoln and her husband and children. She was a hard-working and completely devoted wife and mother. This does not mean that she was easy to live with. There were human frailties in her personality. She had an ungovernable temper and an emotional instability that verged on abnormality; it was to lead in later life to a brief period of insanity. The pitiless strains of a war presidency, the ugly publicity, the loss of her son Willie, and finally the assassination of her husband—these blows were more than a personality so constituted could stand without breaking.

There is the theory put forth by Herndon and Weik, and followed by subsequent writers, that domestic turbulence, driving Lincoln out into the world of men and politics, acted as a spur in his career. Much has been made of his staying out on the law circuit when other men went home on week ends. This is to ignore the fact that Lincoln rode the whole circuit which meant that he was often too far away to get home in days when railroads were just beginning and it was usually a question of going horseback or in a buggy. And the young Lincoln of New Salem who had never met Mary

Todd had demonstrated that the world of men and politics was the world he loved best.

In the whole picture of this marriage the facts remain that Abraham Lincoln and his wife gave each other over twenty-two years of love and devotion. The Lincoln home in Springfield with its beloved children, family interests, mutual ambitions, joys and sorrows, and occasional tempests, was not far removed from the average American home.

In addition to the contribution which Mary Todd brought to the marriage in her background and connections, she introduced her husband to Southern life at its best. In the fall of 1847 the Lincolns with their young sons Robert and Eddie visited the Todd home in Lexington for three weeks, on their way to Washington. Lincoln had been elected to Congress, so it was time for Mary to take him home and show him to the relatives. During these three weeks, Abraham Lincoln had the privilege of living as a member of the family in a typical fine home of the Old South. Though he had visited his friend Joshua Fry Speed in Louisville in 1841, he had had few such experiences. On this 1847 trip and during a visit of several weeks in

[23]

1849, he had opportunity to observe Southern feelings and attitudes and to comprehend how the people of a distinctive region react to conditions that must be viewed from the inside to be understood. Lincoln was accepted by the Todd family, who put certain of their legal matters into his hands. He made yet another visit to Lexington in 1850 in connection with the settlement of the Parker estate.

There was considerable litigation in the Todd family. One of the darkest aspects of slavery was brought home to Lincoln in a lawsuit concerning an octoroon slave girl with a child in whose veins ran the blood of the Todds. This complicated story is told by William H. Townsend in his delightful and scholarly book *Lincoln and His Wife's Home Town.* Mr. Townsend shows how completely the institution of slavery could be viewed by Lincoln on these visits to Lexington. The Todd house servants were held in a privileged and beautiful relationship. "Chaney was in undisputed control of the kitchen; pompous old Nelson ruled the stables with a high hand, while black Mammy Sally, despot of the nursery, gave orders to the little Todds, which even their mother did not dare revoke."

Lexington exhibited varying phases of slavery. In one corner of the public square stood the slave auction block, in another corner the whipping post. Frequent gangs of slaves were taken through the town on their way to slave markets in the deep South. From the home of Mrs. Lincoln's grandmother, Mrs. Parker, one could see the slave jail of a Negro dealer, with dismal slavepens in its yard. Records show that a hundred and fifty slaves went on the auction block within the probable dates of Lincoln's visit in 1849.

Mary Todd knew all the aspects of slavery from what she had witnessed and from the political discussion she had heard in the Todd home. Emilie Todd Helm, her sister, is authority for the statement that Lincoln discussed all important topics with his wife. Mary Lincoln's approach was that of the governing class of the South. From his wife through the years in Springfield and from his visits to her old home in Kentucky, Lincoln had unique opportunity, not only as to slavery but in other matters, to know and understand the mind of "the people on the other side of the line."

One could even speak of Lincoln's political views as Southern. Coming from Kentucky and southern Indiana he could be correctly described in his Illinois period, at least down to the late forties, as a Clay Whig, which meant that he was at one with the large and influential brotherhood of Southern Whigs. Lincoln was a party man and the Whig party was his lodestar. While in the legislature of Illinois he was the leader of the Whig element in that body and would have been elected speaker of the House if the Whigs had gained control. While in Congress he was the only Whig from Illinois, and taking it altogether, he may properly be called, at least for a considerable period, the most outstanding of the Illinois Whigs.

One should not pass too lightly over this Whig significance. In favoring Clay and Harrison before the slavery question became a disruptive force, and, which is more, in favoring Taylor, Louisiana plantation owner and slaveholder, in 1848 after the territorial question as to slavery had been crystallized in the Wilmot proviso, Lincoln was true to Southern Whig form. He continued true to Southern Whig form in favoring Scott in 1852. If he slipped somewhat in his enthusiasm for Clay, his early hero and ideal, he came through with an elaborate eulogy of that Kentucky leader in 1852.

When one bears in mind the strength and distinction of the Whig party in the South, especially on the more aristocratic level, when one remembers that Lincoln stayed with that party from its beginning in the thirties till its disintegration in the fifties, and when one recalls further that Lincoln, antislavery though he was, preferred the Whig candidate to the Free-Soil leader in 1848, one must see that in his political background he had a great deal in common with many of the South's distinguished leaders and many thousands of its voters. As a Whig he was an ardent worker in a party that regularly chose its presidential candidates from the South and that could never possibly hope to win the presidency except with wide Southern support.

Far back in New Salem days Lincoln had looked politically to the South. He did this when in the thirties he attentively read such newspapers as the Louisville *Journal* and the *Missouri Republican*. The latter was thoroughly Whig as long as the Whig party lived. According to Mentor Graham (letter to Herndon, May 29, 1865) young Lincoln's "text book was the Louisville Journal," of which he was "a regular subscriber." Lincoln's ardent support of Taylor in 1848, as well as his whole service in Congress, brought him into intimate touch with Southern members in that body.

He belonged to an organization known as the "Congressional Taylor Club"—otherwise known as the "Young Indians"—which included Alexander H. Stephens and Robert Toombs of Georgia, William Ballard Preston, John S. Pendleton, and Thomas S. Flournoy of Virginia, Edward C. Cabell of Florida, and Henry W. Hilliard of Alabama. Stephens wrote: "I knew Mr. Lincoln well and intimately." In later days of sectional stress it was natural for Lincoln as troubled presidential candidate to address letters to Nathaniel Paschall, editor of the *Missouri Republican,* a Whig paper which never became Republican, and to George D. Prentice, editor of that stalwart among Whig organs, the Louisville *Journal.*

In becoming a Republican Lincoln forfeited that political harmony between North and South which was natural and obvious so long as there was a Whig party to which he could belong. Yet in the troubled fifties when parties were changing and signs of conflict growing, Lincoln still looked South in wistfulness for the old Whig days. If ever a man's reorientation was painful it was so in Lincoln's case. In 1855 he wrote to his Kentucky friend Joshua F. Speed, roommate and good fellow of earlier days, defining his position as to slavery and politics, and giving a revealing glimpse into his disturbed mind in those times of shifting horizons. As to political action, he wrote, "you and I would differ." Yet not "as much," he added, "as you may think." There was a poignant note in Lincoln's wish to keep this Southern friend in political agreement as in personal affection.

✗ He wrote to Speed of their differences on the slavery question not in terms of emphasizing Northern abolitionism; indeed, it was quite the contrary. As to his own personal feelings, it is true, he did show that he was tormented when he saw slaves shackled with irons, as he and Speed had seen them on a steamboat trip in 1841 from Louisville to St. Louis. He confessed that he hated "to see the poor creatures hunted down and caught and carried back to their stripes and unrequited toil." At the time of these experiences he had written to Speed's sister expressing the same views and showing his revulsion of feeling to see "negroes . . . strung together . . . like so many fish upon a trot-line . . . separated . . . from the scenes of their childhood, . . . and going into perpetual slavery. . . ." There was no emotional indifference to slavery in this notable letter to Speed in 1855; Lincoln indicated that he could not fail to have an interest in a thing "which has, and continually exercises, the power of making me miserable." The emphasis that he placed on this reference, however, was that despite antislavery feelings which pained him every time he touched "the Ohio or any other slave border," he would only bite his lips and keep quiet. He was not challenging the Southern right to their institution. He went on to say much of Kansas, then so overstressed in party strife, but added that if beaten on the Kansas question he would acquiesce and would not seek on that account to dissolve the Union.

From the depths of a suffering Whig soul in the days when the Whig party was no more, he wrote: "You enquire where I now stand— . . . I think I am a whig; but others say there are no whigs, and that I am an abolitionist— When I was at Washington I voted for the Wilmot Proviso as good as forty times, and I never heard of any one attempting to unwhig me for that. I now do no more than oppose the *extension* of slavery. I am not a Know-Nothing— That is certain. How could I be?"

One could write a chapter concerning this letter to Speed. Lincoln did not like being unwhigged. When the Republican party was taking shape he would have preferred that old party lines should hold and that Americans North and South should adjust differences within political organizations that extended across sectional lines. Partisanship was bad enough, but partisanship tied up with sectional antagonism was disastrous. Lincoln would have wished to remain in a party that had Southern support. So far as Northern concessions were necessary to produce such harmony, he was ready to make concessions, save only as to slavery in the territories; and even as to Kansas he was ready to consent if it should become a slave state. One can read a certain pathos between the lines as he closed the letter. He mentioned that his wife would pass a day or two in Louisville in October; he sent his kindest regards to Mrs. Speed; he noted that on the leading subject of the letter he had "more of her sympathy than . . . of yours"; he signed his name with far more than usual fervor: "Your friend forever."

Lincoln, who seldom revealed himself to anyone, had opened his heart to the Speeds. Joshua had been his most intimate friend; in a notable series of letters in 1841 he had spoken with remarkable freedom to this man of affairs of the heart. It was in that year that he made an extended visit to the Speed home in Louisville from which he returned greatly refreshed in mind. There were elements both playful and sentimental in his relation to this family. As to the playful, he had shut up Mary Speed in a room to prevent her committing assault and battery upon him; as to matters of deep feeling, besides exchanging intimate confidences with Joshua, he had received from the mother of Joshua and Mary the present of an Oxford Bible which he promised to read regularly after his return to Springfield as "the best cure for the blues."

These were the dearest of his friends, but by 1855 disruptive politics had gone so far that on the matter of parties and on the artificial issue of slavery in Kansas he and Speed were at the parting of the ways. It was the same with other Southern friends, and Lincoln found it hard to bear. He wrote to his comrade in plain words, leaving no doubt of his position, but he wrote with genuine regret; he argued to convince Speed that their differences could be resolved; in any case he was determined that their personal friendship should not be clouded.

✗ It is an oversimplification to say that Lincoln was antislavery and leave it there. Relativity was a big factor. There were degrees, orders, and

[32]

grades among antislavery men. Leaving John
Brown aside as eccentric, criminal, and untypical,
we may note in extreme antislavery ranks such
uncompromising souls as Garrison, Weld, Phillips,
Gerrit Smith, T. W. Higginson, and Theodore
Parker; but Garrison's following was negligible
and the whole combined Northern support given
to abolitionists was exceedingly small. Though this
may be hard to realize, the word "abolitionist" in
the antebellum North was comparable to the
present word "communist" as a hate-word—a
term of scorn, derision, and devastating disrepute.
One who doubts this assertion may take the
episode of the abolitionist debate among students
at Lane Seminary in Cincinnati in 1834, resulting
in the mass departure of students after their
abolition society had been abolished by Seminary
authorities. Gilbert Hobbs Barnes, authority in
this field, quotes a contemporary Northern comment that "abolitionism was regarded as the
climax of absurdity, fanaticism and blood." To be
an abolitionist in antebellum days was to be without political influence and to be widely despised in
the North.

Coming down the antislavery grades we find
different steps and levels. There was John Quincy

Adams, who faced threats of expulsion and censure as congressman because he upheld the right of antislavery petition; but he had upheld slavery in international matters while Secretary of State and was so far from abolitionists as to become a target of their attack. There was Charles Francis Adams, whose genuine but limited antislavery views were promoted on the harmless level of "Conscience Whigs" and "Free-Soilers" rather than of abolitionism. There was Edward Bates of Missouri, who favored free soil and opposed slavery, but who kept his antislavery views within the eminently respectable bounds of border-state moderation and Whig conservatism. There was Kentucky-born Orville H. Browning of Illinois, who disliked slavery and even championed the Negro slave in Illinois courts, but who drafted the resolutions of the Illinois state Republican convention in Bloomington in 1856 with the calculated purpose of renouncing radicalism and catering to conservatives.

When one considers these grades he can better comprehend where Lincoln stood. Rejecting the fanaticism of John Brown, he indignantly denied that his party had any implication in the Harpers Ferry enterprise. He bracketed Brown with

Orsini, who had attempted to assassinate Napoleon III. When a number of Republicans to their later sorrow signed a statement endorsing *The Impending Crisis* by Hinton R. Helper, Lincoln gave no such endorsement, though he deplored the partisan use of the Helper bogey as if approval of this book were the deadliest sin. Lincoln was not so forward for free soil as Chase or Charles Francis Adams. He went as far in conciliation as one could go while remaining an opponent of slavery. Moderation exceeding his would be hard to find among any leaders of his day who had convictions against human bondage. In this respect he was not outdone by those double-distilled Whigs, Browning and Bates.

But what of Lincoln's house-divided statement and his debate with Douglas? Over and again he explained this declaration, indeed almost to the point of explaining it away, as leaders must often do with a pithy, quotable phrase that becomes a bothersome stereotype. Lincoln did not intend that the slavery issue must divide the country. He thought of a peacefully continuing Union, as his very words in the house-divided speech indicated. In this normally continuing Union he looked for a future day when uniformity as to slavery would

[35]

exist in the antislavery sense, but he did not demand disunion while it should not exist. To the extent that the opposite meaning may have been read into his house-divided declaration Lincoln even regretted that he had ever uttered that phrase. He confessed as much. In debate with Douglas he pointed out that in his half-slave–half-free speech he did not say he "was in favor of anything"; he was making "a prediction only—it may have been a foolish one, perhaps." He did not retreat from his house-divided declaration in the sense in which he meant it to be understood; but he did deplore the misrepresentations directed against him and did all he could to check the effort to make it appear that he was stirring up sectional strife.

He agreed that diversity of state institutions was desirable, but as to territories—future homes of free men—he insisted that they be kept free not only for white men and black men, but, as he said with a fling at nativist intolerance, for "Hans, and Baptiste, and Patrick, and all other men from all the world." That he favored a policy, however, did not mean that he would disrupt the nation if he did not have his way.

It would be a mistake to overplay the debates of

1858 or exaggerate the differences between Lincoln and Douglas. No such fundamental oppositeness of position in public leadership was shown in the Illinois senatorial canvass of 1858 as in the great constitutional debate of 1830 between Hayne and Webster. To use another comparison, the 1858 discussion showed no such effort toward a clear presentation of issues shorn of party politics as in the bipartisan teams that went about the country in 1943 to build up popular support for American participation in an international organization to prevent war.

Lincoln and Douglas were stumping the state of Illinois with all the fanfare and fireworks of Western campaigning, the fervor of their agitation suggesting a prairie fire; but in practical policy on most points they were not committing themselves to the advocacy of opposite things. The debates were spirited to the point of being at times overwrought, but they were exceedingly limited in scope. The contending candidates were far from giving a rounded discussion of such questions as might be expected to come before the United States Senate. Their declarations were chiefly concentrated on the narrow but dangerously emotional issue of slavery in the territories. Even on that limited theme there was a believe-it-or-not feature in the fact that Republicans in Congress in early 1861 voted to admit certain territories without any prohibition of slavery. Thus two and a half years after the debates Douglas could truly taunt them with having made a loud party issue in the fifties and then abandoning the issue and virtually adopting Douglas's Kansas-Nebraska position, for which Douglas, while taunting, praised them. The reference here is to congressional legislation in February-March 1861, when laws were passed with Republican votes organizing the territories of Colorado, Nevada, and Dakota on the pattern of Douglas's policy rather than Lincoln's.

x   Had an effort been made in 1858 for Lincoln and Douglas to work out an agreement, they could have found much common ground. On fundamental race relations they did not differ. Lincoln made this clear. Neither favored social or political equality for the white and black races, though in coming years Lincoln's view was to undergo some modification as to political rights. Lincoln did not favor dehumanizing the Negro, but neither did he then favor Negro suffrage, while he referred to such matters as social equality, intermarriage, and the like as "false issues." He even said ". . . I am not in favor of negro citizenship" (E. E. Sparks, ed., *The Lincoln-Douglas Debates of 1858*, p. 303).

Besides agreeing essentially as to white and black relations (though every effort was made to have them *seem* opposites), Lincoln and Douglas both favored letting a Western community decide the slavery issue for itself at the point of becoming a state. Both supported the fugitive-slave act. Neither stood pledged against new slave states. As to abolition in the District of Columbia, though Lincoln had favored this in 1848 in the most conservative and gradual terms, he said in 1858 that he did not "stand to-day pledged" to such abolition. It was not an issue for which he was then agitating. Their only remaining difference after each tried to impale the other on the spikes of formal interrogation (at Ottawa and Freeport) was that Douglas favored a policy by which Kansas would have reached freedom on the road of popular sovereignty (in which he courageously differed from Buchanan and suffered grievously for it), while Lincoln wanted Kansas free by congressional prohibition (though in this very can-

vass Lincoln's party in Illinois was acting in co-
operation with Buchanan Democrats, who were
seeking to entrench slavery in Kansas).

The discussions did not follow the procedures
of purest debate wherein each speaker takes a
position opposite to his opponent's, sticks to the
question, shapes the argument as a progressive un-
folding of issues, notes what his opponent says,
and shows the people how, on matters likely to
come before the Senate, he would take a stand
contrary to that of his rival.

If the Lincoln-Douglas debates lacked greatness, which is the impression one gets if he tries to
read them in their voluminous entirety, it was because on both sides they were actuated by the
motive of party advantage. Lincoln could not dis-
sociate himself from a party that was purely sectional, and we have seen in his letter to Speed how
this fact troubled him. His fundamental friendliness to the South was not adequately appreciated
in an age when parties were too much emphasized
and when factional strife was tending toward civil
war; but good will toward the South was none the
less present in Lincoln's mind.

If the people of the United States could have
by-passed sectionalism in the 1850's, if they could

have treated slavery in the territories and similar questions as themes of statesmanlike adjustment instead of exaggerated partisanship, if they could have kept Whig and Democratic patterns instead of seeing a new sectional party founded while the historic Democratic party was unhappily divided, such a picture of North-and-South harmony would have suited Abraham Lincoln. He did not create the party limitations and frustrations within which unfortunately he had to labor. After he went into the Republican party, because the Whig party was dead and he had to go somewhere, Lincoln was notable among those Republican leaders who tried to avoid tendencies that were called "ultra"—i. e., anti-Southern.

It was because of his attitude of reasonableness in North-and-South relations that Lincoln was nominated for the presidency. The Republican mood in 1860 was that of caution. It was far indeed from antislavery extremism. The Republicans wanted votes; they wanted to win; having won, they did not want the nation to explode on their hands during their party's administration. Perhaps they were too inept to prevent the disaster they did not want. The purpose here is not to argue the controversial question as to how far theirs was the responsibility for the American tragedy. Opposing arguments on this subject were elaborately marshaled in 1930 in a debate between J. G. de R. Hamilton and Arthur C. Cole. One can read them in the *American Historical Review* for 1931 and 1932.

There were five leading aspirants for the Chicago nomination of 1860: Seward, Cameron, Chase, Bates, and Lincoln. None of the five was a radical—not even Chase, though he was more advanced in free-soil views than the others—but it is also true that none of the five was farther from radicalism than Lincoln. No one single factor determined the choice. The excitement of high destiny, deafening yawps in the Chicago wigwam, trading and bargaining, midnight labors of managers among the delegates, the German-American factor, and the weaknesses of each of the other four, had to do with Lincoln's choice. Policy at Chicago was patterned by party managers, not by reformers; these managers issued a harmless platform which disappointed the crusader Joshua Giddings because of its hesitations touching the Declaration of Independence.

The Republican party had not the slightest prospect of Southern support, in spite of Virginia delegates at the convention and some "Texas delegates" who came from Michigan. Nevertheless, in choosing Lincoln they named a man who had spoken often, as at the Cooper Union in that very year 1860, in favor of the greatest friendliness for the South. On that occasion Lincoln said:

A few words now to Republicans. It is exceedingly desirable that all parts of this great Confederacy shall be at peace, and in harmony one with another. Let us Republicans do our part to have it so. Even though much provoked, let us do nothing through passion and ill temper. Even though the Southern people will not so much as listen to us, let us calmly consider their demands, and yield to them if, in our deliberate view of our duty, we possibly can.

It cannot be said that there was clear seeing as to Lincoln and the South in 1860–61. The sequel of his election was a colossal tragedy. In the many things that call for attention in these few lectures, some must call in vain; and in that category we may place the whole secession crisis and the Sumter outbreak. Lincoln's role in that great frustration of statesmanship has been treated by the author elsewhere. (*Abraham Lincoln Quarterly*, March 1940; see also *Mississippi Valley Historical Re-*

view, June 1940.) The stumbling into needless war in 1860–61 was not a matter of elemental causes or genuine interests. Valid interests demanded peace. There was in that hour enough good will in the country if it could have been tapped. The United States is, and was, a Christian nation. Why should Christian good will be placed at so great a discount? Why are people afraid they will be laughed at if they count on harmony among nations? Why are spreaders of ill will stupidly regarded as "realists"?

Lincoln was not making speeches in that period, but if one looks into his important letters—most of which were unfortunately confidential—it will be found that he realized the existence of human friendliness. This theme of fundamental harmony was heavily underlined in his inaugural of March 1861. If the men of politics had worked toward harmony instead of toward disunity, misrepresentation, and hatred in those misguided days, who will doubt that the "needless war" to use George Fort Milton's words—or the "repressible conflict" as Avery Craven has aptly called it—could have been averted? Liberals are insufficiently bold. Christians often lack the confidence of their faith. Constructive democracy is too apologetic. Men of harmony and reasonableness are too often frustrated and beaten. We have heard of sales resistance. There is practical need for hate resistance and for unreadiness to follow the unenlightened politician's lead. In Lincoln's day the imperative need of such resistance was general; it was not limited to one section. Assuredly it was not confined to the South. Zach Chandler, for instance— "Xantippe in pants," Michigan's gift to intolerance—belonged to the "needless" though unfortunately not to the "repressible" category. Chandler was the complete opposite of Lincoln. It was largely in the North that Lincoln's opposites were found, though that is not to say that such opposites were typical of the North. To be exact, Lincoln's opposites were the extremists on both sides.

Lincoln was a Jeffersonian liberal. Clay meant much to him in party guidance; Jefferson meant far more in political and human fundamentals. From his youth Lincoln had given thought to the elements of democratic society. He did not merely burble about democracy. He saw perils. He presented democratic ideals not as spread-eagle generalizations but as part of the tough realities of life. Speaking to a young men's lyceum in 1838 at the age of twenty-nine, he foreshadowed a statesmanship that was liberal precisely in the sense of being realistic. Referring to the edifice which the fathers had reared, he recognized that it was for his generation to transmit the heritage unprofaned. He sharply censured the rough-and-ready lawlessness of his own day, denounced mob law, warned of furious passions, and deplored the violence into which frontier vigilantism had degenerated. He referred to the throwing of printing presses into rivers and to men dangling from trees like the Spanish moss of the forest. He asked every man to remember that to violate the law is to "tear the charter of his own and his children's liberty." It was from the quarry of sober reason that he would hew the civic temple. "Reason . . . unimpassioned reason," he said, "must furnish all the materials for our future support and defence." There was more of Euclid in this man than of Demosthenes. A substantial essay could be written on Lincoln the tough-minded liberal realist.

His Jeffersonian approach was shown many times over—in his emphasis on popular education (for which Hamilton seems to have cared little), his worshipful reverence for the Revolutionary fathers, his equally important recognition that the

Print by F. H. Bresler, Milwaukee

LINCOLN IN 1860

Taken at Springfield in June 1860 by the Chicago photographer, Alexander Hesler. A remarkable contrast to the 1865 picture shown on a later page.

Revolution was over and that evolution was the country's need, his zeal for the Declaration of Independence, his dislike of the "mud-sill theory" that hired workers must always remain on a depressed level, his eloquent pleas for the dignity of labor (in whose ranks he included himself), his championing of the farmer, his oft-stated trust in the rightness of the people. In 1854 he used the word "politician" in the sense of statesman (in which for the moment he may not have been a realist) ; in that sense he declared that Jefferson "was, is, and perhaps will continue to be, the most distinguished politician of our history."

Lincoln was, of course, conservative in his dislike of the "radicals" of his day; but these radicals were themselves reactionaries, so that Lincoln's opposition to them must be counted for liberalism. He understood the meaning of democracy only in the liberal sense. We may truly call it the Southern liberal sense: it would have been acceptable to a Willie Jones, a John Taylor of Caroline, a George Mason, or a Thomas Jefferson. The friendliness of Lincoln toward the colored people was a Southern type of friendliness, as shown in his affectionate regard for William Florville ("Billy the barber") and in Mrs. Lincoln's kindness to colored servants. This is one of the enduring folk traditions of the colored people. Their love of the Lincolns is deeply personal.

In earliest life, in years of growth, in love and friendship, in the family circle, in the tough substance of democratic thought, Lincoln's mind and character were molded by Southern influences. In wistfulness for other days when sectionalism was raging, in the midst of tragic strife as at Gettysburg where he uttered not a syllable of hatred, Lincoln gave evidence of Southern understanding. In his closeness to border-state opinion, in his design for freedom, in incidents of presidential helpfulness to friends on the other side, and at the last in his pattern for peace without vindictiveness, Lincoln kept his sympathy for the people of the South.

II

LINCOLN AND THE SOUTHERN BORDER

IF WE may speak of one salient feature that ran through Lincoln's presidency, it was the theme of an antagonistic dualism, a clash of opposites. It was radicalism versus moderation; unctuous rebel-baiting intolerance on the one hand, moderating human relations on the other. It was Olympian denunciation versus friendly adjustment, partisan interference versus constructive rebuilding. It was Frémont versus Kentucky. One found this counteraction of men and measures everywhere. It was inescapable. It was the recurring motif in the Lincoln drama. Turn where he would, Lincoln could not find relief from it. It gave him sleepless nights; it pervaded his administration; it was bound up with the ultimate frustration of his long-time program.

This dualism was no side issue. It touched fundamentals. It was not a matter of ordinary routine or of casual action. It was a matter of aims and objectives, of the very cause itself. If Lincoln thought of the purpose of the war—or rather of statesmanship looking through and beyond war—the conflict of radicals versus moderates was there. One group said: Produce, or reproduce, a Union in which the restored South could be satisfied. The other group said: The South is wicked; let them suffer for their crimes; make sure they do not escape suffering even by returning to the Union; make doubly sure that they do not endanger the Republican party. In some of its forms the degree of war bitterness was unbelievable. That is what war does.

To see clearly through all this bitterness, to hold vindictives in check, to remember future objectives amid maddening wartime complications, called for a high order of statesmanship. To keep the border within the Union involved so much that it almost comprehended the totality of Lincoln's main problem. In the strategy of politics and in the selection of commanders the great border had always to be watched and studied. In the many-sided aspects of emancipation, in the making and shifting of the

President's cabinet (which at the outset contained two border-state men but only one New Englander), in the choice or rejection of punitive measures, and finally in the construction of peace, this border issue with all that was focused therein, comprised one of the most important and controversial of the questions of Lincoln's rule.

It is well to remember what the border was. In viewing the whole country it is as inadequate to think merely of North and South as to believe that all the teeming interests of the great nation were bound up in sectional squabbles concerning slavery. From the standpoint of interests, ideals, and regional distinctness, Avery Craven (*Coming of the Civil War*, p. 5) has called attention to seven areas in the Lincoln period: the Greater New England, the Ohio Valley, the Old Northwest, the Blue Grass regions, the Lower South, the Southwest, and the Prairies. Giving a further analysis of the regions, Mr. Craven reduces them to four: the Northeast, the Old South, the Northwest, and the Southwest. He shows that these major sections were "not entirely unique or entirely separate." Disruptive sectionalism, climaxed in the crisis of 1860–61, was not the basis of either of these groupings, but even if one takes that basis the sections would not be merely two. They would be at least four: lower South, upper South, the broad border, and the North. Of these four sections, three were Southern or predominantly so.

If we may indulge in a play upon words, the border area was medial; it was also intermediary and mediating. It was not a region of ingrowing sectionalism. It was a link, not a barrier. The border had friends on both sides. The upper South resembled the border, which in turn had much in common with large contiguous regions in the North. The medial region served not as one who separates enemies but as one who introduces friends, not as a buffer state but as a bridge between the Cotton Kingdom and the Yankee world. If some overruling power could have selected a part of the country to give the answer as to peace or war in 1860–61, the Kentucky region would have performed in such a capacity better than a region at one of the extremes. In the turn that events took, Kentucky was denied its true role.

It is striking, almost startling, to take the Southern or Southward-looking area that remained within the wartime Union and note its immense proportions. The Union-supporting area whose people and habits were Southern included, according to Edward Conrad Smith (*The Border-land in the Civil War,* p. 3), a white population of 4,967,000, as compared to 5,094,000 within the Confederacy. Here one should carefully note that Smith's border area is construed to include only Kentucky, Missouri, "Western Virginia," and the southern portions of Ohio, Indiana, and Illinois. He gives convincing reasons for treating this as a homogeneous area. If, however, one adds Maryland, which is commonly recognized as a border state, one then finds within the Union a broadly Southern region whose white population exceeded that of the Confederate South. Thought patterns, modes of life, tones of speech, and political attitudes in this great area give far more reason to call its men and women Southern than to call them anything else. If one doubts this, let him move about among these people today—for instance, in southern Illinois; let him also study their history.

Human factors and conditioning influences enable one to appreciate, perhaps to predict, the action of a people, so far as that action is not artificially forced. So it was with Kentucky. Here was a state whose people were Southern, while at the same time they were entirely content to stay within the Union. That Union had been and remained fundamental in their thinking. Leaders of the state, from Clay to Crittenden, had been compromisers and adjusters. When divisive sectionalism raised its head, Kentuckians had not been out in front shouting threats, but behind the scenes trying to work out solutions. They had no motive to withdraw from the United States; it was equally true that they had no wish to fight or coerce their Southern brethren. In the unhappy days of the growing crisis they moved from support of Bell in the election of 1860, through the Crittenden compromise, to the advocacy of a border-state convention to be held in the Kentucky capital for the prevention of war. In the early phase of the secession movement, when calling a state convention would have been understood as promoting disunion, Kentucky refused to call a convention. The Frankfort convention which it did call, and which was intended to draw a number of states together in co-operation, was for the opposite purpose.

For such a people the mid-April explosion in 1861 was intolerable. It produced a sense of frustration, severe shock, and startled incredulity. If asked to invoke peace, Kentucky could do that. To hope for winning back the lower South seemed not impossible. What did seem impossible was to face the dilemma of Sumter and of Lincoln's call for Kentucky militia to be used against seceded areas. The fate of Americans of that day, the cruel dilemma of war, was bound up in the plight of Kentucky. Her people had plenty of fighting spirit. Her men as individuals, if it came to the worst, would make their choice, even though it was only choosing so as to be with the right set, which young Henry Watterson confessed to be his motive in entering the Confederate army. This personal dilemma was bitter enough, but a greater difficulty was to know what to do as a state. Sumter meant utter negation of Kentucky's purpose, which was not merely to maintain the Union, but to do so without war.

Kentucky had a policy. It was essentially the same as Virginia's: preservation of the Union by consultation, compromise, and peaceable adjustment. Devices intended to implement the policy were somewhat different. The Virginia legislature called what was intended to be a convention of all the states, though when it met in February 1861 at Washington the Peace Convention merely contained representatives from about two thirds of them. The Kentucky legislature very late in the game (April 3, 1861) passed a resolution for "a convention of the border slave States, and such other slave States as have not passed ordinances of secession, to meet at Frankfort, Kentucky . . . ." By this action of the legislature Kentucky delegates were to be instructed "to consult [with delegates from other states] on the critical condition of the country, and agree upon some plan of peaceable adjustment." The date for this border-state convention was set for May 27, which in itself practically amounted to complete frustration of the whole well-meant effort. The convention was actually held on May 27, but with only Kentucky and Missouri represented and with little accomplished except strong affirmation of Kentucky's Unionism.

Union-conserving compromise with avoidance of war was the common ground of Kentucky and Virginia, as it was in general of the upper South and the border. For that matter, there was considerable sentiment in that direction in the deep South. Events moved too rapidly, however, both in lower Southern secession and in the Sumter crisis, to allow this policy to develop. Moderate men like to proceed by talking things over, by a meeting of minds. They move slowly. They permit discussion. They allow dissenting groups to be heard. They give time and unhampered opportunity for militant or even subversive groups to organize. Too often moderate men are at a disadvantage compared to bold men who move quickly to the point where the very door to adjustment is closed and locked. This closing and locking meant the collapse and defeat of Kentucky's basic program. It came as the rudest interruption at the time when the implementing of their program was the preoccupation of Kentucky leaders. People of the state were looking vaguely to Frankfort when others were looking impatiently to Montgomery.

Reorientation in mid-April came hard to border minds. The Sumter debacle left Kentuckians with no place to go. Instead of offering a solution, it dashed to the ground every hope of a solution in Kentuckian terms. For border policy to have succeeded, war had to be averted. Once war was started, the whole orientation was changed. To avert the war would have been a high achievement. Instead of that, Kentucky was asked merely to take sides and fight it out. That taking sides was to come after an interval, but during that troubled interval neutrality was the natural immediate wish. It was not that neutrality, which implies war, was Kentucky's preference. It was simply that complete frustration of the border program could not be too quickly followed by belligerency. Even after Sumter the border wished pathetically for a retracing to the days when peace seemed yet possible. From such a retracing the people of America seemed psychologically inhibited and congressionally unadjusted, but to accept this inhibition at the first startled moment was asking too much. If Sumter was the casting of the die, then it was all over so far as Kentucky's true contribution was concerned. But in the minds of dazed human beings there was an unwillingness to believe that the die had been cast.

Neutrality for Kentucky did not mean retreat into a bomb-proof cellar because of unreadiness to fight for a cause. Not at all. It did mean that in mid-April 1861 a prolonged four-year horror could not be prospectively envisaged. If war was started, perhaps it was a false start. Who could know? Why should the fifteenth of April be so devastatingly different from the fourteenth or the eleventh? Why, merely because of Sumter, should the hand of war control the whole nation's coming destiny instead of the hand of peace? Had measures of adjustment been in fact exhausted? Did the country intend to drop so unpremeditatedly into fraternal strife? Why should an incident produce a war? Why should a step, or misstep, toward human slaughter be the irrevocable thing and peace the unrecoverable thing? Neutrality meant that Kentucky still stood ready to invoke peace by trying to call it back from the immediate yesterday. It meant that a border state, a commonwealth of the South and of the pioneer West, with many sons in the Northwest, wished to keep out of the war that it had no part in producing, wished to keep the war out of Kentucky, and wished, as the Frankfort convention demonstrated, to continue the days when adjustment was yet practical. If this meant hoping against hope, that at least was as good as hopeless despair.

Neutrality meant also a necessary *modus vivendi* for a commonwealth in which Union and Confederate camps were forming, with recruiting on both sides, internal agitation raging, families and villages split apart, and newly enlisted soldiers in opposite services traveling on the same train. It meant a kind of truce. Perhaps it was something like an armistice at the beginning of the war. If there had to be a fight, time was needed for squaring off before blows were struck. If it was war, it

[59]

was usually conceived as war outside Kentucky. Actual shooting would come after men had spread themselves a bit in their new uniforms, certainly after they had been in camp and training. To have to shoot down your neighbor of the next farm because you were on the same train though headed for opposing camps was not contemplated. Even the warmakers did not want the war to come too close.

Neutrality ultimately proved so impossible that it now seems wishful thinking. The neutral course could not produce peace; when peace was lost, neutrality could not recall it. Kentucky was to realize that prevention of war is too big a matter for one state, just as men of the present generation have realized too slowly that a nation cannot have peace merely by wanting it. Neutrality is only a wartime device by which it is hoped that involvement will be avoided, but Mars has an arrogant way of controlling things once he is let loose. Whether a nation will become involved depends on events, not upon the will to neutrality.

Demands of peace are great and challenging. In the choice of peace or war there is a startling contrast between popular desire and official performance, between the wide and valid support for peace and the inadequacy of governmental instruments and leaders to maintain it. Conversely, the contrast is between the invalidity of the warmaking few and the terrific power which that few wields. To realize the tragedy of this, one must remember that the many do not have to use their force in actual shooting; they have only to be ready, organized, and determined to do so. There is a maddening paradox in the whole situation, for it is by trying to avoid involvement that a nation may be dragged into the waging of a war. It is by failing to use the peaceful strength of many states that the warmaking few may set the pattern for a continent or a world.

Kentuckians were not to blame in 1860–61. The state's own course was high-minded. Kentucky was simply part of a faulty American system which did not adequately protect the peace and did not make effective the pacific desires of the country while giving a disproportionate effectiveness to troublemaking groups. The holding of a fully competent national convention soon enough, with full co-operation of the outgoing and incoming administrations, might possibly have been the answer. Instead of this, conventions called by Virginia and Kentucky failed to fulfill their peace-making purpose while for the larger task reliance was placed upon Congress, which was not even called into special session and which failed to bring adjustment. That was one of the greatest congressional failures in American history.

As to Lincoln's attitude toward this huge border region, one finds a paradox: Lincoln understood the border people, but they did not understand Lincoln. In his office of President, Lincoln had to reckon with the border. He had to take it into his every calculation. Yet it was a region in which he had but the weakest support. Lincoln could not expect the border people to favor his party or be attached to his administration. There was no chance of that. He had therefore to assume that people in this region would make a distinction between the Republican party and the Union cause. (In the long run and in the general picture an opposite stereotype was being fabricated: the Union cause, especially in later years, was represented as synonymous with the Republican party.) Lincoln once remarked, we are told, that he "had very little influence with this administration," meaning his own. He had to accept border opposition to what was called his administration while seeking border support for causes and measures that looked beyond a presidency to the continuing nation.

He could not win his war for the Union without remaining wedded to the border, no matter how difficult the domestic adjustments of this marriage. To lose Kentucky, wrote Lincoln to O. H. Browning (September 22, 1861), is "nearly the same as to lose the whole game." "Kentucky gone," he added, "we cannot hold Missouri, nor, as I think, Maryland. These all against us, and the job on our hands is too large for us. We would as well consent to separation at once, including surrender of this capital." On the military side, if Lincoln had lost Kentucky the Ohio River would have been the boundary between contending sections. If such an event had allowed Confederate forces to enter the region and seek early control, fortifying the river from Cairo perhaps to Maysville, to say nothing of the political implications involved, the situation would have constituted a serious threat to Lincoln's cause. If he had lost Maryland, the capital itself would have been surrounded. If the border had gone all-out for disunion, the task at home and abroad, as Lincoln viewed it, would have

[63]

been hopeless. He had to have Kentucky; yet Kentucky had given him less than one per cent of its vote in 1860.

Some, at a distance from Kentucky, viewed the whole question in terms of crisis psychology. It was right against wrong, they would have said. Kentucky was wrong for hesitating, for not taking sides, or for helping the wrong side. Kentuckians in 1861 had to endure the taunts of these men, while at the other extreme they had to endure taunts from the deep South to the effect that they were motivated by fear and were submitting to Federal cóercion. But this type of crisis psychology was no better than its premises. It was altogether too naïve to suppose that any one group of states or any one party had a monopoly of the right. In a nation of thirty-four diverse states and in a historic situation where North and South had shared the profit of slavery, the wrong thing was warmaking, and the right thing was adjustment, especially since slavery in the states of the South was not actually in question. Right and wrong could not so easily become a matter of latitude.

In judging of Lincoln, however, one judges in terms of his sense of the destiny of the United States. Without attempting a pontifical answer on a question concerning which Americans have fought and died it is sufficient for the present purpose to note that this pattern of the nation's destiny in terms of the continuing Union, without self-righteous claims or imputations, was for Lincoln the main question, and that it was intimately bound up with the border issue.

In the five months after Sumter Kentucky moved uneasily from peace plans to Magoffin's indignant refusal of Lincoln's April call for militia, then to neutrality (officially announced by the legislature in May), and from that by troubled stages to the expulsion of Confederate forces and finally to the placing of the state squarely though uncomfortably on the side of the Union. This was Kentucky's transition, and psychologically a period was necessary for the change. In these troubled months Kentuckians could not be pushed either way. That very fact could help the Union, but only if the Union cause were skillfully handled.

In this interval very few of Kentucky's outstanding leaders favored carrying the state over into the Confederacy. As for John C. Breckinridge it would be truer to say that in 1860 he was the secessionists' candidate than that he himself was a secessionist. The office for which Breckinridge was presented in 1860 was that of President of the United States. He was, of course, the candidate of the secessionists—of Wigfall of Texas, of Yancey of Alabama, of Rhett of South Carolina—but he was also the candidate of President Buchanan, of the New York *Herald,* and of many thousands of Unionists in the North and the border. It has happened before, and since, that a presidential candidate has been supported by diverse, or even diametrically opposite, groups. Breckinridge's editorial supporters represented him with vigorous emphasis as supporting the Union. "The charge of disloyalty to the Union against Mr. Breckinridge," declared the *Kentucky Statesman* of Lexington (August 28, 1860), "is as false and infamous a slander as ever emanated from a political pen." The Richmond *Examiner* declared on October 26, 1860: "They [Breckinridge's opponents] cannot say that any principle or measure advocated by Breckinridge . . . will be used to destroy the constitutional Union of these States."

Breckinridge remained in the United States Senate after the Sumter crisis, assailing Lincoln and denouncing his "usurpations," but declaring his lifelong attachment to the Union. His elaborate Senate speech of July 16, 1861, instead of showing interest in the cause of secession, showed indignation toward Lincoln and his party while expressing also the great lament that compromise had failed. After this, Breckinridge entered the Confederate military service, being one of those Southerners who did not go with his state. His service in the United States Senate was terminated by expulsion, but it was part of Breckinridge's record that he professed loyalty to the Union in which he believed. When he left it, the Union had already been broken. Had he been elected President, he reasoned, the Union would have been sustained. Of the 53,000 votes which Breckinridge received in his own state in 1860, by far the major portion were probably cast with a Union-preserving intent, just as all the votes for Douglas, as well as the state's predominant vote for Bell, were cast in that sense. Kentuckians had voted for Breckinridge not as a secessionist, but as a Kentuckian, a favorite son, a Southern Democrat, and a supporter of the existing Democratic administration.

Kentucky's governor, Magoffin, vigorously opposed Lincoln and showed a greater friendship for the secessionist element than was acceptable to his people; but he supported neutrality, resented Con-

[67]

federate interference, and stepped out of the picture, yielding to Robinson, when neutrality gave way to Union adherence. Of Kentucky's other leaders, the most prominent in political life were supporters of the Union. Cassius Clay was not typical; he was a Republican, an upholder not only of the Union but of Lincoln. Crittenden hoped that Kentucky would continue a neutrality that might one day lead to reunion of the sections. Venerable James Guthrie, railroad promoter, outstanding Democrat, and former Secretary of the Treasury under Pierce, having hoped and worked for compromise, placed himself and his railroad on the side of the Union; in postwar days he favored the Lincoln-Johnson plan of reconstruction. Garret Davis, successor of Breckinridge in the United States Senate, followed the Clay road into full support of the Union, as Guthrie had followed the Jackson road to the same goal. Bramlette took a commission in the Union army, becoming Union governor of the state midway in the war. Robert J. Breckinridge was an "unconditional Unionist" and became Lincoln's chief supporter and adviser on Kentucky affairs. George D. Prentice was vigorous for the Union, as his Connecticut background might lead one to expect.

Other Kentuckians who stood for the Union were Benjamin H. Bristow, Joseph Holt, James Harlan, John M. Harlan, and the Speed brothers—Joshua F. and James.

Despite this Union wartime stand, a curious, though understandable, thing happened to Kentucky after the war. It has been fictionally suggested by a moving picture in which Will Rogers, portraying a typical Kentuckian, said in postwar days: "We fought for what we thought was right," meaning they had fought for the Confederacy. Kentucky as a state had in fact kept with the Union. Its Confederate soldiers had been far less numerous than its Union soldiers. Yet after the war the attitude that seemed "right," romantic, gentlemanly, psychologically satisfying, Kentuckian, and successful in vote getting, was the attitude that went with a Confederate record. Historical reality to the contrary notwithstanding, the thing on which Kentucky wanted to pride itself in tradition and in retrospect was the Lost Cause. Yet it was cherished not so much as a cause; rather as a memory. Feeling for the cause was not combined with true regret that it was lost. It was as if Kentucky retroactively and sentimentally joined the Confederacy after Appomattox.

[69]

Lincoln showed himself a diplomat in his handling of the Kentucky situation. He did not rush proceedings or force the issue. Much of his Kentucky policy was handled behind the scenes, by messenger, by conference, by influences centering in Cincinnati, by word of mouth, or by confidential statement. He used conciliation without selling the Union cause down the river. He maneuvered to exhaust his opponents' trumps, but only by playing the game. He listened to protests from the other side, even restraining his own supporters lest they become too ardent or premature in action. When he wrote a paper on Kentucky affairs, in this difficult April-to-September period of 1861, it was couched in language that would reassure and satisfy, yet make no stultifying commitment. So long as Kentucky committed no active resistance to the Federal government, he preferred to avoid provocative action; yet he declared his intention of enforcing the laws so far as he was supported in doing so by the people of the United States. His Kentucky policy was such a balancing of delicacy with firmness, of delay with watchfulness, of Unionism with self-determination, that he, as much as any man, must be given the credit for keeping Kentucky. Since he considered holding or

[70]

losing Kentucky the equivalent of gaining or for-
feiting the cause itself, the keeping of this state,
viewed from the Union standpoint, was no small
achievement. From the Confederate standpoint
the Kentucky development was regrettable; it constituted the loss of an important trick.

When on June 30, 1861, the people of the
state voted for members of the Federal Congress
—choosing between opposing parties labeled
"Union" (not "Republican") and "State Rights"
—nine of the ten districts showed a majority for
the Union candidate. In a total of 130,000 the
State Rights candidate received only 37,000 votes,
considerably less than one third. In interpreting
this election it must be remembered that neither of
the terms "Union" or "State Rights" was self-
explanatory. If state rights meant joining the
Confederacy, that could hardly be consistent with
voting for a member of the Congress at Washington, and in fact many Kentuckians of the Confederate persuasion did not vote at all. (Since,
however, the total popular vote in Kentucky for
President in 1860 had amounted to only 146,000,
the number of those who deliberately refrained
from voting because of Confederate sympathies
could not have constituted a very great element in

the state.) Unionism, it is true, could have been explained as signifying little more than neutrality. Admitting this, it was important to Lincoln to have those Kentucky congressional votes. He did not expect Republicans from this area, but by not expecting everything he got something; in fact, he felt greatly encouraged by the results of this election.

The Union cause held good also in other parts of the border. In Delaware and Maryland secession was avoided and the Federal government substantially supported. In eastern Tennessee Union sentiment was strong, though a separate-state movement in that area was frustrated. In a situation that was *sui generis* and bound in legal shallows, the northwestern counties of the Old Dominion set up their state of Virginia, shifted its capital from Wheeling to Alexandria, then created a new state which they thought of naming "Kanawha" but which entered the Union with the name of "West Virginia."

There is evidence that Lincoln disapproved of the partition of Virginia, which was not necessary for the support of the Union cause in that area if one were to regard the Pierpoint government as valid. Gideon Welles recorded in his diary on

December 12, 1862, that Lincoln considered the creation of a new state "of doubtful expediency" at that time. In the diary of O. H. Browning, three days later, there is a reference to a conversation in which Lincoln talked of the West Virginia bill, expressing himself as "distressed at its passage." Lincoln's Attorney General, Edward Bates, not only opposed the creation of the Mountain State; he mentioned it (e. g., in his diary of October 12, 1865) with scorn and scorching sarcasm.

Yet Lincoln signed the West Virginia bill, as he signed other bills which he did not like but which were favored by those who controlled Congress. The President even issued a public paper justifying the admission of the state to the Union. He admitted, however, that such action was "dreaded as a precedent." He excused it by saying that "a measure made expedient by war is no precedent for times of peace." His reasoning on the subject showed him a capable lawyer, but the historian knows that his argument, which came simultaneously with his presentation of the emancipation proclamation to the cabinet for final revision, did not reveal his inner doubts. Lincoln did not like a quarrel with Congress. Sometimes he by-passed Congress in his public measures, but seldom did he

[73]

lock horns with the lawmakers. He was not a veto-
ing President. People of the time were thinking of
West Virginia as a gain for freedom, and Lincoln
would partly have spoiled the effect of his emancipation proclamation if he had vetoed the West
Virginia bill which Congress had passed after a
remarkable and spirited debate. It was the events
of the time, however, rather than his own
preference, that produced his reluctant approval.

Missouri resembled other border areas, but
with some differences. Missouri had many Ger-
mans; it had Republicans; it had a border on Iowa
and another on Kansas; it had St. Louis, which was
a military center in the West; it had Frémont; and
it had Mrs. Frémont. The state was a battle-
ground between opposing forces so intermingled
and so complexly interlocked that the struggle
could not be considered merely as a regular war or
a conflict of armies in the usual sense. Perhaps
none of the states manifested so strikingly the
governmental disruption, private feuds, irregular
tactics, ambitious jealousies, sniping, guerrilla
warfare, popular excitement, pervasive turbulence,
and contending governmental structures that ac-
company civil war within a state. It would appear
that internally Missouri was the most violently

upset of all the commonwealths in the war period, as perhaps Louisiana was the most internally disturbed of them all in the period misnamed "reconstruction."

As for Frémont, he almost reached the stature of Poland as a troublemaking issue. If Frémont was mentioned, people took sides, and they did so immoderately. If Lincoln had handed affairs over to Frémont, he might as well have given up the basic purpose of his struggle for a reunited country rather than a sectionalized government. Frémont was hasty, incautious, dashing, impulsive, colorful, vigorous, unbending, and a bit superior in his attitude toward Lincoln. He was more than a man. He was a name or a symbol. He was the darling of the abolitionists, the pet of the radicals. He was whitewashed by the congressional committee on the conduct of the war.

A balanced over-all view of public affairs was never Frémont's forte. He was precisely the type that could become the tool of fanatics. He was anti-Lincoln in the whole trend of his wartime career. Known as the great pathfinder of the West, and without talent as a military leader, he was early in the war thrust into the position of highest Western command. The Department of the West which he commanded with headquarters at St. Louis was a widely extended military sphere that comprised many states, included the great inland rivers, and reached potentially far into the South. It controlled the earlier stages of those decisive military operations that came to be associated with U. S. Grant.

The United States had a President, and Missouri had a governor—or rather two of them, one Union and the other Confederate—but Frémont reached out for civil as well as military power; and on August 31, 1861, he issued a stirring proclamation in which he "assumed the military powers of the State," whatever that meant. He proclaimed martial law throughout Missouri, ordering that persons taken with arms in their hands be shot if convicted by court-martial. The property of persons hostile to the United States he declared confiscated; their slaves he declared "free men." Here was military emancipation proclaimed by a general without presidential authority. Here was a ringing battle cry for abolitionists. Here was swift punishment for rebels; here to many was a Joshua ready to lead the hosts of the Lord.

The shower of bouquets that greeted Frémont's order from one direction and the avalanche of curses from the other produced for Lincoln his most disturbing internal problem since Sumter. August of 1861 was an early date in the Lincoln administration and in the unhappy war for an episode in which radical men became openly anti-Lincoln men. Agitation was intense and praise of Frémont was self-righteously extravagant. Welles of the cabinet was informed that gentlemen from middle western states "unanimously" approved Frémont's proclamation. This could have been true only of some; it was obviously not true of the people as a whole in that region. Letters pouring in to public men from radical-minded sources gave the impression of Frémont as a knight in shining armor who was saving the country, and of Lincoln as a blunderer and a tool of the slavery interests.

On the other hand, Lincoln knew that the Frémont agitation was the worst possible complication for the delicate Kentucky situation, which was at that very time heading toward solution in terms of Union adherence. To approve of Frémont, he felt, was to lose Kentucky and the border, as well as to abandon his basic idea of a long-run moderate policy toward the South. Martial law, confiscation, and emancipation were not matters to be handled by proclamations of an impulsive

[77]

general. They were far-reaching issues to be handled by Congress and the President. Lincoln simply had to overrule Frémont, who had become involved in a feud with the Blairs and whose management of affairs at St. Louis had been marred by charges of graft, overbearing military swank, and inefficiency. At first Lincoln gave Frémont the chance to revoke his own order. That being refused, Lincoln himself overruled it. Then as complications multiplied, Lincoln after patiently seeking to get along with the Frémonts finally came to the point of removing the general from his Western command.

He explained this action to Senator Browning. The proclamation of the general amounted to "dictatorship." It was not for a general, he said, to confiscate property and to fix the permanent future status of slaves. It amounted, he said, to assuming "that the general can do anything he pleases." Lincoln stated that the "Kentucky legislature would not budge till the [Frémont] proclamation was modified" and that he could not lose Kentucky. Yet the President explained that it was not merely because of Kentucky that he acted as he did concerning Frémont. What he probably meant was that essential points of large policy were focused in the Frémont-Kentucky controversy, and that he could not allow Frémont and his agitating supporters to force the presidential hand on fundamental solutions.

It is sometimes said that Lincoln went over to the radicals, but this is far from true. Radical opposition to him became an increasing crescendo of bitterness in the later years of the war. In the Frémont matter he put his foot down in the antiradical sense. He kept the border states in the Union, which he could hardly have accomplished on the basis of any surrender to the radicals. He did not get all the border-state support he wanted, but perhaps he got all that the cards allowed. He endured abuse for the sake of holding the border. He took pride in reporting to Congress the number of Union soldiers furnished by Delaware, Maryland, Kentucky, and Missouri. He kept a strategic eye upon operations in the West. When uneasiness for Kentucky subsided, Tennessee became a kind of specialty with him in this respect. When he reached the point of proclaiming emancipation he did not apply his edict to border states. Men of the border were given important appointments, though there was always the danger that acceptance of patronage from Lincoln would prove an embarrassment. Mrs. Ben Hardin Helm, sister of Mrs. Lincoln, was specially befriended, though her sympathies were with the Confederacy, for which her husband gave his life. For the hard job of rebuilding a broken nation, attention to the middle area helped the nation's chief to steer a middle course.

All told, Kentucky and her neighbors had great significance for Lincoln. That significance was a matter of birth and boyhood, native hills, underlying origins, marriage, cultural ties, close friendships, and challenging problems in the field of statesmanship. To subtract Kentucky with its influences and with it the huge border area is to leave out much of Lincoln's personal life and public history.

III

DESIGN FOR FREEDOM

A SUITABLE text for this lecture might be the statement of an old Alabama Negro a few years ago. When questioned about Lincoln, he said: "I don't know nothin' 'bout Abe Lincoln 'ceptin' dey say he sot us free, an' I don't know nothin' 'bout dat neither." The old darky's saying might apply to many among our worthy citizens, though perhaps few of us could quite match him in the wisdom of admitted ignorance.

To say that a thing is "well known," as is the emancipation proclamation, often signifies that virtually everyone has heard of it, but signifies little more. People have heard of "free silver," or "freedom of the seas," but how many persons selected at random could state informatively and correctly what these "well-known" terms mean? Emancipation during Lincoln's time and after is a subject which can only be understood after considerable study. It is a topic on which uninformed generalizations miss the mark by many leagues. The freeing of the human slave is as far from being generally understood as the freedom of the seas or the freedom of silver.

At the time of its issuing the emancipation proclamation was referred to from one standpoint as the act of a fiend, from another as pointless and futile, and from still another as the coming of the Kingdom of Heaven. Everyone who has heard of Lincoln has heard of the proclamation; yet of Lincoln's ponderings concerning the institution, of the complexities of his policy, of his long delay, of presidential action that seemed the opposite of freedom, and of the main design for liberation in Lincoln's mind there is a vast and widespread ignorance. As to the constitutional and legal obstacles involved, few people are competently informed. Limitations in the famous proclamation itself, with its definite lack of a kingdom-come quality, produce a sense of amazement.

Lincoln was never an "abolitionist." He was antislavery in sentiment and principle, as were many nonabolitionists, but what he believed was one thing, while what he conceived to be his duty as President was quite another. "If slavery is not wrong," he thought, "nothing is wrong." He had always felt so, but by every measure of what Lincoln was and what the abolitionists were, he was not one with Gerrit Smith or Theodore Dwight Weld. He never even joined the Liberty or Free-Soil parties, limited as their objectives were, much less the abolitionists. He did not clamor for imposing abolitionism upon Southern communities. Garrisonian immediatism was far indeed from his policy. He did not ignore the social adjustments and realities that emancipation involved. He did not abuse Southern slaveholders as wicked persons. He thought in long-range terms. He was content that liberation should come slowly, and he greatly preferred that it should come by the action of the Southern people and states. When it should come, he favored compensation of slaveholders by the United States government for the taking of their property. He not only favored this; he considered it ethically sound. If it was a matter of guilt as to the institution, he specifically said that the North and South must share the blame. They had shared the responsibility for slavery as well as the profit; it was, in his view, only right that the financial burden of removing it should be commonly borne.

Wendell Phillips spoke of Lincoln in disparaging and belittling terms. William Lloyd Garrison thought him comparable to a "wet rag." Count Gurowski, the wild-eyed Polish-American whose radical sympathies found sizzling expression in his diary and letters, wrote: "You cannot change Lincoln's head, you cannot fill his . . . empty skull with brains." At another time the growling Count declared: "Lincoln acts . . . [only] when the gases of public exasperation rise powerfully and strike his nose."

Such quotations could be vastly extended. Comments on Lincoln by abolitionists, if assembled at length, would constitute an anthology of abuse. Abolitionist radicals of the prewar, wartime, and postwar era were the precise opposites of Lincoln. In reading the competent chapters of *Lincoln and the Radicals* by T. Harry Williams, we find in page after page how these vindictives sneered at Lincoln, blamed him for everything that went wrong, interfered with his military conduct of the war, assailed his tenderness toward slavery, praised the men who were causing him embarrassment, tried to unhorse him, invented false charges against the commander of the Army of the Potomac, pilloried capable generals, sought to put their own pets in military command, resented the President's attention to Kentucky, criticized him as being too lenient toward the South, and wished eagerly for another man in the White House.

Rightly to present the subject of Lincoln and emancipation would be to review the whole elaborate wartime history. Almost every main issue had its bearing upon slavery. At home, problems of the enslaved race presented constant complications. In international affairs, as shown afresh in Jay Monaghan's *Diplomat in Carpet Slippers,* emancipation came to be regarded almost as a kind of secret weapon to win the war by gaining foreign sympathy. On the military side, questions of escaping slaves, of Negro troops, and of radical politics in its effect upon the army, presented many an aggravating challenge.

Lincoln's liberation policy grew by stages. It was the product, not the producer, of events. In the first phase Lincoln was like John Quincy Adams, who in his own view opposed slavery, but who as Secretary of State under Monroe had always to remember that he was the foreign minister of a great slaveholding nation. Lincoln himself said he did not consider that the presidency conferred "an unrestricted right to act officially" upon his "judgment and feeling." He felt rather that his presidential oath forbade him "to practically indulge . . . [his] abstract judgment on the moral question of slavery."

There is no intention here to argue whether the war rose because of the slavery question. To analyze that issue would be undertaking too large a task. The wretched war arose because of a complex situation in which misunderstanding, false propaganda, overbearing agitation, timidity, misplaced defiance, precipitate action, and blundering were considerable factors. Lincoln headed a party that disclaimed any intention of hitting slavery in the states, and Lincoln himself made this disclaimer for his administration in his inaugural of 1861. In so doing, he was mindful of his responsibility as Chief Executive rather than of his individual view or preference. He was mindful also of the wish in a serious crisis to place and keep the slavery question where it belonged—as a domestic institution to be modified, kept, or abolished according to governmental decisions, not as a supreme nuisance in the field of parties and politics or an explosive menace threatening the life of the nation. Often the true statesman must remember not only that "force is not a remedy" as John Bright said, but that a difficulty facing a nation—whether it be slavery in 1860 or Poland in 1945—may become either a test of statecraft or a choice item for troublemakers. There are those, of course, who prefer the menacing approach. Where a subject is at once exceedingly difficult and potentially dangerous the statesman finds his greatest task at precisely the point where the agitator finds his readiest opportunity. Of those who wanted slavery to continue to be a nuisance and an explosive menace rather than a problem for adjustment it can be said that they existed on both sides; it can also be shown by the record that the desire for moderation on both sides was Lincoln's chief concern.

He did all he could in his inaugural to reassure the South. He offered protection, as he said, "as cheerfully to one section as to another." He did not enter office with the concept that he was merely President of the North or merely of the Republican party. Congress as well as the President put itself on record as disclaiming any intent to overthrow the "established institutions" of the states, declaring in the Crittenden resolution of July 22, 1861, that the war was not to be promoted otherwise

[87]

than for maintenance of the Constitution and the Union.

These disclaimers marked an early phase of a shifting situation. Particular Negroes, escaping into Union lines, knew little of the Crittenden resolution or of the President's inaugural. War over a vast front produced unpremeditated incidents that would not fit themselves into a neat pattern of letting slaves alone. As incidents multiplied, in a subject too elaborate for present treatment, Congress took piecemeal action here and there, so that by the time of the preliminary emancipation proclamation of September 1862 Congress had done a number of things affecting slavery. The nation's armed forces were forbidden to restore escaping slaves to their masters; such slaves, if their masters were hostile, were declared free on coming within Union lines; slaves of Confederates were declared free (second confiscation [or treason] act, July 17, 1862); and slave-soldiers, with their families, were included in congressional liberation. Out-and-out emancipation by Congress was considered without being adopted; but the liberating provisions of the second confiscation act, a clumsy and ineffective piece of legislation, were even more far reaching than the emancipation proclamation soon to follow.

In addition, in April 1862, Congress abolished
slavery in the District of Columbia with compensation and colonization; two months later the lawmakers at Washington prohibited slavery in the
territories, a deed which the Supreme Court said
they had no right to do. In the international field
the Negro republics of Haiti and Liberia were recognized (even American-sponsored Liberia had
not received recognition before this); and in May
1862 the United States joined with Great Britain
in a treaty of co-operation to suppress the international slave trade.

  In these earlier phases Lincoln devoted a great
deal of his thought to his main policy of liberation
—i. e., to a scheme of conservative, voluntary,
gradual emancipation to be encouraged, not forced,
by the Federal government, and to be accompanied
by colonization of freedmen on distant shores and
Federal compensation to Southern slaveholders.

  If one were to ask what was Lincoln's design for
freedom, this was it: not forcible immediate abolition by executive edict, not the blowing of a utopian
trumpet, but recognition of the rights of slaveholders, caution in legal matters, deference to the
states, financial remuneration to be borne by the
United States government, and gradualism reach-

ing forward to the year 1900. The fact that his plan fell through has caused Lincoln's advocacy of it to be somewhat slighted except in the more ponderous historical accounts. His attention to colonization, and to the two abortive efforts to put it into effect, is a somewhat unfamiliar subject. One of these colonizing efforts, or projects, was in Central America, the Chiriqui location; the other was on the *Ile à Vache,* off the island of Haiti and belonging to that republic. The utter impracticality of giant-scale deportation of freed Negroes, as shown in these hapless experiments, leads us to wonder why Lincoln's practical mind should have given so much attention to them.

What is perhaps even more surprising, to those who think in familiar terms of the Emancipator, is the unflattering comment and disheartening advice given by Lincoln to a deputation of colored men who met him at the White House on August 14, 1862. What Lincoln told his dark friends on this occasion, when he pointed out the disadvantages of their remaining here even under freedom and the advisability of settling abroad in areas whose salubrious climate he recommended highly, was like a dash of cold water to those who thought of emancipation as an easy cure-all.

In the main—i. e., except as to the District of Columbia—Lincoln got nowhere with his scheme of compensated emancipation, but his repeated urgings on the subject show a persistence and a deep emotional earnestness which were almost pathetic. Lincoln thought that his plan was a comprehensive scheme to shorten the war. More than that, he thought of it as a great national measure to deal in statesmanlike terms with slavery. To answer those who were afraid of the cost he showed in detail how by a quicker ending of the war it would save money. He presented his program as a method of ridding the country of an outmoded institution in unprovocative terms that would recognize slaveholders' rights and invite peaceable Southern co-operation. He wrote voluminously on the subject to Congress and gave his best legal thought to the drafting of a bill for emancipation in Delaware. The plan, however, was more suited to peace than to war; it required state and Federal co-operation which was not then forthcoming; it envisaged a constitutional amendment; and it would have necessitated something which was for the most part nonexistent under Lincoln—teamwork between President and Congress.

Meanwhile as time passed it seemed to antislavery enthusiasts that Lincoln's voice often sounded more like that of Pharaoh than that of Moses. When some of his generals—Frémont in Missouri and Hunter in the deep South—issued unauthorized edicts of military liberation, Lincoln disappointed many good souls by overruling their orders and insisting that the slavery problem be controlled at Washington. When his unco-operative Secretary of War, Simon Cameron, included in his annual report of December 1861 a passage advocating the use of slaves as soldiers, Lincoln caused advance copies of the report to be recalled and a new expurgated edition to be issued, thus enhancing the importance of the unhampered "Simon-pure" article. When Greeley appealed for antislavery action in his "Prayer of Twenty Millions," Lincoln came through with a balanced and restrained letter in which emancipation was subordinated to the Union. When a church delegation from Chicago pressed upon him a demand for liberation, he talked against a presidential proclamation of freedom, comparing it to "the Pope's bull against the comet." Having said this much he sought to restore the balance, if only slightly. It is sometimes forgotten that he tried in his concluding remarks on this occasion to reassure the earnest brethren from Chicago, hinting that the whole matter was "under advisement," but certainly the main tone of his response was negative and non-committal.

It was after such hesitation, avoidances, negative pronouncements, unsuccessful efforts toward voluntary state action, and studies of constitutional procedure that Lincoln issued his preliminary proclamation of emancipation in September 1862. The fact, not known at the time, that his decision to do so had been reached in July made the intervening months especially difficult for a harassed President who had the document reposing in his desk drawer but who had to choose the time for issuing it, meanwhile giving out statements of a contrary or colorless nature. This desk-drawer interval was also in the Union view one of the gloomiest and most hopeless periods of the war in the military sense. McClellan, who had kept Lee occupied near Richmond, was for no good reason displaced by Pope, whose failure brought a victorious Lee and Jackson to the gates of Washington. It is difficult fully to recover the darkness of those critical days, the utter desperation and panic at the nation's capital caused by Pope's crushing defeat at Second Manassas. In the nick of time McClellan at Antietam gave

Lincoln the marked military improvement that was indispensable for prestige abroad, for emancipation at home, and for much besides, including Lincoln's very position.

In issuing the proclamation of emancipation Lincoln took a step which he had disclaimed the intention of taking in his inaugural address of March 1861, but he did not look upon this as a repudiation of a promise. The pledge not to interfere with slavery in the South was made within the pattern of the United States, to apply to states in the Union. It presupposed continuance of peace; it was an assurance that leaving the Union was not necessary in order to retain state autonomy as to slavery. The pledge of March 1861 could have been paraphrased: Remain in the Union and you can keep your slaves. When the proclamation came in 1862, it could have been paraphrased: Remain in the Union, or return to it, and you can keep your slaves. Adherence to the United States was the principle that conditioned Lincoln's planning. His inaugural declaration did not amount to a prophecy of what his government might do in case of war. Such a prophecy would have been out of place, hypothetical, and provocative. In the grave hour of Lincoln's first presidential utterance no one who knew him could think of convicting him of insincerity. Had conditions remained as Lincoln then envisaged them, there would have been no presidential edict of emancipation.

When wartime emancipation was adopted with great reluctance, the President could have taken the ground that the past should not control the future, but there was more than that. He had given his policy of noninterference with slavery an extended trial of seventeen difficult war months before the preliminary proclamation was issued; at the time of issuing he reiterated the compensation offer and provided a warning period of a hundred days before the proclamation should go into effect. He had urged without success his design for compensated emancipation by the states. Even in time of war, and in a situation in which John Quincy Adams had once said that slavery would have to fall before the war power, Lincoln had tried for many long months to live with Southern slavery as he had before the war. He wrote: "After the commencement of hostilities I struggled nearly a year and a half to get along without touching the 'institution'; and when finally I conditionally determined to touch it, I gave a hundred days' fair notice of my purpose to all the States and people, within which time they could have turned it wholly aside by simply again becoming good citizens of the United States." On April 4, 1864, Lincoln wrote: "I aver that, to this day, I have done no official act in mere deference to my abstract judgment and feeling on slavery."

Lincoln was striking, however "conditionally" and imperfectly, at a constitutionally protected institution; but he felt that the alternative was that of "surrendering the Union, and with it the Constitution." There were, of course, those who differed with him, North and South, on this matter; but to understand his approach one must remember that he said: "I could not feel that, to the best of my ability, I had even tried to preserve the Constitution, if, to save slavery or any minor matter, I should permit the wreck of government, country, and Constitution all together."

He made a point of justifying the emancipation edict as a war measure, but it is worth while to note in what sense he used this justification. By recognizing that war does unusual things, a leader avoids the implication that drastic instruments are cheerfully or wantonly used. After all his hesitation Lincoln had acquired an air of confidence and even a sense of divine destiny when the instrument was actually used. He was placing many limitations upon the measure but he knew his mind in intending to go ahead with it. He developed this decision not from any cabinet advice, but from his own pondering of complex war problems. It was his own. Perhaps no act of his administration was more so. He knew that he had to lift the measure out of a normal constitutional setting in order to justify it and to do this without seeming to disparage or disregard constitutional procedures. He was careful to speak of the edict as a "fit and necessary" war measure; by linking it with the whole cause of Union success he spoke as a President reluctant to do arbitrary things, as one who would take an unprecedented action only because he believed after long study that he could not avoid it in a desperate emergency.

In almost every phase of the Lincoln subject one finds contradictions or seeming paradoxes, and one should not be too much surprised to note the contrasts between Lincoln's confident assumption of power and his evident feeling that the proclamation was unsatisfactory. He was bothered by some of the aspects of his edict. One could almost say that he did not like his most famous act. We have seen that he had called it a "bull against the comet," that he had waited a long time to do the deed, and that he had spoken more than once in the contrary sense. Events did it, not himself, he said. The slavery question did not remain static in dynamic times. The war was posing issues that could not be dodged.

He thought deeply of the duty of doing a thing whose legality was not clear. He did not conceal his legal doubts. Speaking on January 31, 1865, he said: "A question might be raised whether the proclamation was legally valid." He therefore favored a constitutional amendment as "a king's cure-all." When on December 8, 1863, he announced his program of reconstruction, suggesting an oath of future loyalty as a step toward restoration, the oath-taker was asked to swear to abide by laws concerning slaves, and also to support presidential proclamations in the same field "so long and so far as not modified or declared void by . . . the Supreme Court." Why did Lincoln put this in? Possibly because of his sense of the sanctity of an oath; perhaps he did not want those who had solemnly taken his oath "in presence of almighty God" to be troubled in conscience later because of having sworn to support something which the Supreme Court might conceivably declare void.

It is most unusual for the Court to declare a

presidential proclamation void, but Lincoln was contemplating that very possibility. The fact that such a voiding by the high Court was considered possible was one of several indications of Lincoln's uncertainty concerning the law-worthiness of his liberating edict. Toward the end of the war, at the Hampton Roads conference, Lincoln went very far in admitting legal insufficiencies in the emancipation proclamation. When asked as to its postwar effect, he said he did not know and could give no answer. It was a judicial question, he said. It was his own opinion (as reported by Alexander H. Stephens) that the proclamation was a war measure; therefore it "would have effect only from its being an exercise of the war power." When the war ceased: ". . . it would be inoperative for the future. It would be held to apply only to such slaves as had come under its operation while it was in active existence." (This he said by way of indicating that the question was in doubt. He did not know how the courts would decide it.)

What did Lincoln's emancipation proclamation accomplish? To answer this question in terms of immediate efficacy would be to reduce the accomplishment to nothing. Of all traditional stereotypes, one of the most unhistorical is the illusory concept of Lincoln the Emancipator sitting in the White House and by a flourish of the presidential pen suddenly striking the shackles from millions of Negro slaves. Reduce the millions to tens, and the concept would still be incorrect. It could almost be said: Lincoln issued his proclamation and nothing happened.

One should note in this connection the exceptions in the two proclamations themselves. By the September proclamation Lincoln still adhered to procedures that were very different from liberation by presidential edict. He gave the restoration of the Union as the main object; he emphasized his purpose still to promote compensated emancipation by the free acceptance of the states; he reiterated his desire for colonizing persons of African descent "upon this continent or elsewhere." Instead of acting then he merely gave notice that freedom would be proclaimed on the first day of the following January in areas then to be designated, such designation to apply only where states or parts thereof should be "in rebellion against the United States." The January proclamation did not provide liberation in any of the Union states; it did not apply to Tennessee; and large areas in Virginia and Louisiana were specifically excepted from its terms. The curious fact is that Confederate arms were in control in the regions to which presidential emancipation applied, while the liberating hand, or pen, was withheld in areas that were under Union control. According to Seward the government was liberating slaves only where it could not reach them. The *Annual Cyclopaedia* for 1863 (p. 835) stated that the proclamation "did not appear to make free any slave by its own operation during the year." As months passed more areas subject to the proclamation were gained by Union arms, but actual implementing of the edict was not provided by any deed or certificate of manumission recognized in the courts; the care of freedmen, such as it was, was left to the varying, imperfect, and improvised practice of military commanders. New Year's Day of 1863 was in point of fact no Day of Jubilee, nor was there ever any emancipation day of general application to all the slaves, nor even to slaves in all the non-Union areas.

To a large extent slavery was still active and legally alive by the very terms of the January proclamation. Slavery was being dealt with piecemeal. The institution was being conserved while at the same time it was being partially proclaimed to be abolished. In the last half of the war, emancipation in Union areas depended upon state action and there was a lack of uniformity among Union slave states as to what should be done. If slavery had a longer life expectancy in some areas than in others, the commercial profits of such a situation would not be overlooked in that profiteering age. When Missouri was working toward emancipation by state action slave traders saw their opportunity. Not only did they buy slaves cheap in Missouri to sell them at a good figure in Kentucky; they kidnapped fugitive slaves, which after all was cheaper, and they seized "contrabands" for whom the proclamation offered no relief. It is an understatement to say that then as now the laws and the courts did not function with complete efficiency in the protection of Negro rights.

How could a particular Negro show that he was free? His life was poor enough at best, but here was his great day. How should it be signalized? To solve this problem a curious suggestion was made in a letter found in the papers of Secretary Stanton under date of December 27, 1862. The writer suggested a medal inscribed "Free Negro" with a scriptural quotation and with the Latin words: *omne ignotum pro mirifico*. (For the benefit of myself, and with the use of a dictionary, I trans-

late: all things unknown are thought to be won-
derful.) If the owner could not read, so much the
better. The author of this plan would have had men
of the dark race go about in by-paths, swamps, and
woods, to distribute the medals, which he thought
ought to be about the size of a quarter so that they
could be easily concealed. He suggested that they
should be made of cheap pewter. Perhaps the plan
was conceived as a kind of psychological warfare
behind the enemy's lines. In any case the plan was
not adopted; it has a curious rather than a significant interest.

To tell how freedom came to Negroes of this or
that locality would be a complicated story. There
has been so much oratory, poetry, and folklore on
the subject that one turns with gratitude to the
competent pages of Bell I. Wiley's *Southern Negroes*. One also finds the subject covered locally in
many scattered personal diaries or biographies and
in state studies for the period, such as that of Walter L. Fleming for Alabama. All history is limited
by time and place, and if one seeks to learn how
freedom came he has to note where the slaves were
and of what period he is writing. Some of the slaves
moved out from the plantation seeking Union
camps or vaguely searching for the freedom they

had heard of; but that was more likely to be true in areas close to Union armies. Most of the slaves, at the point where liberation reached them, were where they had been—with their Southern white people, upon whom they were dependent for daily bread and toward whom they continued to feel a sense of loyalty and family pride. The faithful colored servitor, hiding the silver or guarding his master's family, though now something of a stage picture, has more authenticity than the fanciful stereotype of violent Negro insurrection or the distortions of such a screen drama as *The Birth of a Nation.*

It was in the white household or upon the plantation that the slave belonged. To say that he was now free usually did not mean that his life and status changed suddenly because of decrees at far-off Washington. Washington did not even supply those pewter medals. It did supply the Freedman's Inquiry Commission and the Freedmen's Bureau; but the Commission's function was merely that of a survey, while the Bureau was too much a creature of the War Department and of reconstruction politics to handle the far-reaching problems of emancipation. To Southerners the Bureau seemed an alien thing. Some of its responsible officials—

including its head, General O. O. Howard—were
high minded; but many of its lesser agents were
little more than tools of the Republican party.

A President might proclaim, and Union generals
might set up camps for Negro refugees, but to the
slave the final authority was his master's own word.
As for insurrection against the master, that simply
did not happen. If disorder was found and if mis-
deeds occurred, such irregularities were understandable under existing war conditions; thousands
of white men in those days turned to turbulence and
to defiance of government. "On the whole," wrote
W. L. Fleming, "the behavior of the slaves during
the war . . . was most excellent." As field workers or house servants at home they did their part.
With the armies they dug the trenches and split the
wood. As body servants of Confederate officers
they were faithful unto death. Their minds did not
have a Garrisonian slant. Some of them thought of
a Yankee as a thing with horns. Most of them re-
joiced over Southern victories and wept for Confederate dead.

The last day of slavery and the first day of freedom usually came with little drama. As indicated
by the Latin motto previously mentioned, it was the
unknown in freedom that was admired. When free-

dom came it sometimes led to exploitation of the blacks, as for instance by Union pickets who returned them to their former masters and pocketed the reward. The extent to which Negroes were cheated is one of the sorry stories of the time. It is not pleasant for a historian to say these things. Some writers find glory in the Civil War, but there was a great deal of sordid conduct in that unbalanced time, just as there was a scandalous and discreditable period of partisanship and corruption after the war.

There is not time to recount contemporary opposition to the proclamation. In the wartime South it was severely and indignantly criticized; but a more significant answer from Dixie came when Southern states took their own emancipating steps in 1865, though Lincoln did not live to see it. Some of the Northern slurs on the proclamation, however, were almost as vehement as the Southern. Many linked the proclamation of freedom with the simultaneous presidential proclamation suspending the habeas corpus privilege; often these two edicts were bracketed together in a common protest. Browning opposed the proclamation. Fessenden considered it *brutum fulmen*. A pamphlet in New York declared that free Negroes in the North were "a standing monument to the folly of Abolitionism." There were many who agreed with a Kentuckian in the belief that "abolitionism had to be prostrated" in order to settle the war. Benjamin R. Curtis, formerly of the United States Supreme Court, aimed a stinging pamphlet against the proclamation as a misuse of executive power. The New York *Herald* described it as "a dead letter," "unwise and ill-timed, impracticable, and outside the constitution."

Negative points, however, do not form the whole story. What Lincoln did not do, what Congress and the states failed to do on Lincoln's urging, what the proclamation did not provide, and what it encountered in the way of opposition, have received attention because of the necessity of remembering authentic history. To leave the subject there, however, would be to omit a great deal. Somehow, despite all its limitations, the proclamation did become a force. Perhaps it became more of a slogan than an enforced edict, but as such it had vitality. Freedom was something in the air. Inspirational aspects of the proclamation at the North— or in certain Northern circles—were tremendous. For the stirring of men's souls the war took on new meaning. Good people, Christians, humanitarians, hailed it with delight; their speeches, hosannas, and prayers had an effect upon home morale. It was the Victorian age.

The proclamation was admired at a distance. If it was the unknown in freedom that the slave considered magnificent, it was the vague aura of glory that won the applause of freedom lovers in the North. It was not so much a question of what the soldiers believed as they battled through the blood and stench of war. It was a question of what was said and written back home. A sentimental story by the elder Oliver Wendell Holmes in the *Atlantic Monthly* could produce disgust in the mind of the younger Holmes in the Union army, but the elder Holmes had many readers. Close-up realities and difficult complications of emancipation could be oratorically overlooked. Legal provisions as they would appear in a court were not the main concern of jubilating hearts. It was not a matter of statistics to show how many were freed, nor of sociological surveys to discover what became of them after they were freed. The thing admired was a generalized rather than a particularized freedom. To hold an emancipation meeting furnished a greater thrill than to welcome large numbers of freed Negroes into a Northern community with promises of economic opportunity.

One should look twice before thinking too cynically of all this. People thought of Lincoln as a divine instrument. They thought of something greater than any President, of Providence intervening in the affairs of men, using the rough hand of war to accomplish a holy purpose. That the edict came at New Year's gave it a kind of Messianic quality, a note of ringing out the old and ringing in the new. It was another "Battle Hymn of the Republic." A deed had been done for freedom. God was keeping watch above his own. Something was happening that had to do with Lincoln's fame. World concepts of the man as well as traditional national memories of him were taking shape.

The distressing part comes in when one thinks of a great inspirational force and a spiritual uplift becoming an instrument for abuse. To lofty souls freedom offered a higher goal than national unity. If restoring unity meant preserving slavery, unity would seem an inadequate objective. While to some this might be pure humanitarianism, it might also become a motive to prolong the war and to use the war for partisan purposes. There is evidence that radicals would not have wanted the war to end too soon. They actually did not wish for McClellan to take Richmond in 1862. Motives in those days, especially at the front of political action, did not always come in unmixed purity. From the exalted ideals of true humanitarians to the schemes of party-minded politicians was a far cry; yet the politicians could maneuver things so as to get the support of humanitarians. Radicals desired not only the liberation of black slaves; they desired vengeance upon the South and yearned for a regime of party domination. Freedmen were to be their tools. The concomitants of emancipation got out of Lincoln's hands. He could issue his proclamation, but he could not control the radicals.

In looking forward to the postwar future the best of statesmanship was demanded not only to abolish slavery, but to bring readjustment and enlightened progress in the face of all the intolerant influences of that unhappy time. A leader then had constantly to watch whether partisan intolerance was not the motive with humanitarianism as the cloak. To take a thing so complex and so potentially uplifting as emancipation and to associate it with the hateful spirit of party and sectional abuse would be the worst disservice to the Negro. To enlist for him the helping hands of those nearest to him, those with whom he would have to live, to make freedom one with normal Southern rebuilding, would be the part of statesmanship, but for such statesmanship the times were not suited.

As a man whose mind was open to Southern interests, Lincoln recognized that freedom for the submerged race was the Southerner's problem. Lincoln was never one of those Northern leaders who insisted on dictating to Southerners what they ought to do about their home affairs. He did not overlook the fact that a Southern problem could become a national one, but in such a case he believed its national phases could be handled best with Southern co-operation. It is not too much to say that even in war time he was ready to rely on Southern good will. After his emancipation proclamation he still hoped for state action. In favoring gradual liberation in and by Missouri he wrote on June 22, 1863, that he preferred the process to be gradual rather than immediate. That raised the question whether in the transitional interval from slavery to complete freedom the national government would protect slaveholders and their property. Though aware of the difficulties of the problem, especially as to permitting bondmen to be "sold . . . into more lasting slavery," Lincoln nevertheless believed that "legal rights in slaves during the progress of emancipation" ought to be respected. To promote this policy of friendliness to slaveholders, he would brave abolitionist wrath. Where efforts toward liberation were made in good faith by slave states, he would not thwart them.

On January 8, 1863, one week after his definitive proclamation, he pointed out to General McClernand that things were "as of old" with respect to states not included in that document. He contemplated "systems of apprenticeship for the colored people" and argued that, even where the proclamation applied, the people of the Southern states "need not to be hurt by it." Referring to a dread as to enslaving or exterminating the whites of the South, which he called absurd, he wrote to McClernand that "no man" was "less to be dreaded for undue severity" than himself.

To ease the transition out of slavery was a matter to which he gave careful attention. Writing on August 5, 1863, concerning affairs in Louisiana, and recognizing that there were parts of that state to which the proclamation did not apply, he expressed his wish that the state itself would "adopt some practical system by which the two races could

gradually live themselves out of the old relation
. . . and both come out better prepared for the
new." Such a matter as a "probationary period"
came to his mind in this connection. "Education for
young blacks," he said, ought to be included in the
plan for applying emancipation. He thought also
that the element of contract should be considered,
with emphasis upon "its simplicity and flexibility."
By this he probably meant that different ex-masters
could adopt different types of contract.

How continuously and unbrokenly Lincoln per-
sisted in taking Southern rights into account in the
problems of slave liberation has perhaps not been
sufficiently realized. He did so from the earliest beginning to the very last. His position as to compensation, as well as his whole approach to the
problem of the war and slavery, he summarized
in February 1865 at the Hampton Roads conference. In words recorded by Alexander H. Stephens: "He said it was not his intention in the beginning to interfere with Slavery in the States;
that he never would have done it, if he had not
been compelled by necessity to do it, to maintain
the Union; that the subject presented many
difficult and perplexing questions to him; that
he had hesitated for some time, and had resorted to

this measure, only when driven to it by public necessity; that he had been in favor of the General Government prohibiting the extension of Slavery into
the Territories, but did not think that that Government possessed power over the subject in the States,
except as a war measure; and that he had always
himself been in favor of emancipation, but not immediate emancipation, even by the States."

"He went on to say [wrote Stephens] that he
would be willing to be taxed to remunerate the
Southern people for their slaves. He believed the
people of the North were as responsible for slavery
as the people of the South, and if the war should
then cease, with the voluntary abolition of slavery
by the States, he should be in favor, individually, of
the Government paying a fair indemnity for the
loss to the owners. He said he believed this feeling
had an extensive existence at the North. He knew
some who would be in favor of an appropriation as
high as Four Hundred Millions of Dollars for this
purpose."

Part of the story of Lincolnian emancipation was
the tidal wave of enthusiasm that swept the
British nation as popular meetings were held in
London, York, Halifax, Birmingham, Sheffield,
Coventry, Manchester, Bristol, Bath, Glasgow,

IV

DESIGN FOR PEACE

LINCOLN'S design for peace is a painful subject. The more one realizes how just and promising his plan was, the more tragic does the subject become because of the wrecking of the program by Congress. But before going into topics that are too heavy it may be well to note how matters stood on the level of personal adjustment.

For this purpose there comes to mind an incident in the family of General George E. Pickett. After the fall of Richmond, as the General's wife tells the story in *Pickett and his Men,* a Union army surgeon appeared at the Richmond home of the Picketts, mentioned his friendship for the Confederate general, and offered help. Mrs. Pickett declined it, but later, after her husband joined her and on his advice, the help of this surgeon in the Union army, George Suckley, was accepted. The Picketts were taken in the surgeon general's steamer down the James to Norfolk. Mrs. Pickett relates that her party was then taken up Chuckatuck Creek to her old home, all the way to her father's wharf. Not everything that Mrs. Pickett wrote on the Lincoln theme—friendly and favorable as it was—has been accepted by historians; but this story has a significant point; it presents the off-duty feeling of men who were officially enemies but could not forget that they were in fact friends.

On the part of George Pickett and George Suckley there was the complete absence of even the slightest cloud on the old friendship. They chatted cordially of old days and drank to each other's health. They were joined by General Rufus Ingalls, another dear friend of Pickett. Ingalls and Pickett talked of having slept under the same blanket, fought under the same flag, and made love to the same girls. The Pickett baby was told that he needn't mind "about hating *this* Yankee." Post-war policy for junior also included a piece of candy and the parental admonition never to become a politician. Feeling engendered by the war is not our subject; but if George Pickett and his Union friends had the overpowering wish to discard war-time hatred, to have done with it once and for all, there were many on both sides who agreed with them.

Among them was Lincoln. As President, he had definitely the concept: in time of war prepare for peace. It was not his view that the government should postpone a formulation of its settlement aims till the conflict was over. Winning the war was not enough. To design the pattern of the postwar nation was to his mind the main issue. It was a wartime issue. Let the nation emerge from fratricidal strife on a practical, reasonable pattern —a simple one, without too many *whereas's* and *therefore's*—and Lincoln would have signed the war off. He would have trusted to later years for further development, forgetting the unfortunate past and insisting only on reunion and emancipation. The main factor in his scheme of reconstruction—certainly his opponents would have said so —was leniency. What he deplored was vindictive hatefulness tied up in legislative red tape.

Lincoln's plan evolved through successive stages. In the first phase he acted to discourage carpetbag beginnings and truculent severity in the occupied South. In his letter to Governor Shepley of Louisiana under date of November 21, 1862, he said it would be "disgusting and outrageous" to

send "a parcel of Northern men . . . as representatives" from Louisiana to Washington,
"elected, as would be understood . . . , at the
point of the bayonet." Butler's truculent rule at
New Orleans was an un-Lincolnian chapter. For-
tunately it was comparatively brief; it lasted but
seven and one-half months, from May 1 to mid-
December 1862. The worst possible mistake concerning Butler would be to consider him typical
either of the government at Washington under
Lincoln or of the North. After all, Lincoln did
have the grace to remove him. Other leaders of
Union rule in the wartime South were of a less
provocative character; they were such men as
Banks in Louisiana, Johnson in Tennessee, and
Geary late in the war at Savannah.

In the next phase, in December 1863, Lincoln
launched his scheme of easy reconstruction in a
proclamation that envisaged rapid re-establishment of state governments in the South, not by
carpetbaggers, not by Zach Chandlers, but by the
people of those states. They were asked only to
swear allegiance, restore prewar governments, and
recognize emancipation. Even the acceptance of
emancipation, as Lincoln stated, did not preclude

such arrangements as a Southern state might wish to adopt "in relation to the freed people of such State, which shall recognize and declare their permanent freedom, provide for their education, and . . . yet be consistent as a temporary arrangement with their present condition as a laboring, landless, and homeless class . . . ."

For this purpose, as an initial device, Lincoln would accept as a sufficient electorate a tenth of the votes cast in a particular state in 1860, on the understanding that the tenth (or more) could qualify in two respects: by showing that they were qualified voters before secession, and by taking the prescribed oath in which they were merely to swear future allegiance to the United States and support of emancipation.

This did not mean that Lincoln was promoting minority rule. He was not using a minority to sign away the rights of the majority. So far as his off-hand pattern of Union with emancipation allowed, he was leaving everything to the Southern people. He definitely recommended that, in the re-establishment, the state be restored with its prewar name, boundary, constitution, and code, save only that existing laws and proclamations of the United

States regarding slavery be observed, except as repealed, modified, or held void by the Supreme Court.

For the prewar South it was assumed that a state government rested broadly on its people; under Lincoln's plan a restored government would continue to rest on the people. To get such a restoration set in motion, however, he preferred, in the abnormal situation that confronted him, to act quickly without waiting for majority expression. It has happened before that a popular government has been set in motion by a minority. That was true in the launching of the Constitution of the United States. In terms of a modern figure of speech, Lincoln's plan was that a minority would crank the engine; then the majority could run the machine. He did not foresee the "Model T"; he expressed it figuratively in terms of the egg and the fowl. Another possible figure would have been to say that majority rights were being temporarily administered in trust by a minor portion of the electorate. To hold them in trust was not to surrender or discard them. That Lincoln was proposing an informal initial device was the essential part of the whole subject. In a time of great emergency he was interested in the main practical result; he was not frittering away the whole case while trying to work out a perfect legal formula.

Other phases of Lincoln's plan need not be detailed at this time. He earnestly tried to start his plan working as additional parts of the South came within his reach. His efforts were frustrated. As it turned out, no state was actually restored to the Union according to Lincoln's plan, though he considered his terms fulfilled in North Carolina, Tennessee, Arkansas, and Louisiana. In Florida, though nothing came of it, he had John Hay at work early in 1864 on the oath-taking aspect of restoration. In Virginia he accepted what was called the Unionist "restored government" under Pierpoint which Congress refused to accept.

In his program for generous reconstruction, as in many other matters of his troubled rule, Lincoln was confronted with the hateful opposition of anti-Southern radicals who seized party control and wielded for their factional purpose the power of Congress—a power which is supposed to be wielded for the people. The politicians who checkmated him in matters of reconstruction spoke of him scornfully while he was President and sought to prevent his re-election. One of the early episodes in the reconstruction muddle was the Chase presi-

dential boom, which was a furtive attack upon
Lincoln's leadership. In promoting that boom, as
shown in the "Pomeroy circular," the radicals
showed clearly that they proposed to overturn
Lincoln, whose re-election they declared practically impossible, as well as undesirable because of
"his manifest tendency towards compromises and
temporary expedients."

A yet more bitter challenge to Lincoln came in
the Wade-Davis bill of 1864 and its aftermath.
This bill embodied the radical program of difficult
and ungenerous reconstruction, which is perhaps
enough to say of it, since it was killed by a pocket
veto. In a stinging public "manifesto" Wade and
Davis gave Lincoln the severest scorching, though
they were Republicans and he had just been re-
nominated in convention as Republican presidential candidate. The New York *Times* stated,
August 9, 1864, that the purpose of the Wade-
Davis manifesto was to defeat Lincoln's re-election, and in this very month—perhaps the darkest
of all the wartime months in the North—an amazing movement was promoted within the Republican party which had as its purpose the discarding
of Lincoln and the substitution of another man as
Republican nominee.

If the 1864 phases of peace and reconstruction brought recrimination, factional smirching, and governmental deadlock, the 1865 phases were also, to use a Lincolnian phrase, environed with difficulty. There came in February 1865 the Hampton Roads conference on the steamer *River Queen* anchored near Fort Monroe. Jefferson Davis was not present, but the Confederate government was ably represented by R. M. T. Hunter, John A. Campbell, and Alexander H. Stephens. For the United States the representatives were none other than President Lincoln and Secretary of State Seward.

Personally the meeting was not unpleasant. Small talk was indulged in, reminiscences were exchanged, and it was seen that the war had not destroyed old friendships. The meeting lasted four hours, no one besides the high officials being admitted except a colored servant who brought cigars, water, etc. The Hampton Roads conference failed—i. e., no peace terms were arranged—and at least two factors contributing to this failure may be noted:

(1) The parley was badly muddled from the beginning by the self-inspired visit to Richmond of the elder Francis P. Blair, who conferred with

Jefferson Davis and got the project all tied up with his brainy scheme for war against the French imperial forces in Mexico. Blair's idea was that the Confederate States and the United States should stop fighting each other in order that together they might make war to liberate Mexico. Besides a misreading of the purposes of the Confederate government, this was putting the Monroe Doctrine in a wrong setting. Events were soon to prove that no war was needed to cause French imperial collapse in Mexico. That collapse followed almost automatically when the unpleasantness between North and South ended in reunion, and when the readiness to employ the army to enforce the well-known policy of the United States made the use of force unnecessary. The United States did a better good-neighbor act by letting the top-heavy French structure collapse than they could possibly have done by going in from the outside with liberating armies.

(2) The second point of failure in the Hampton Roads conference was complete disagreement as to its purpose. The government at Richmond expected results, if at all, in terms of an armistice that would suspend hostilities so that the war could be ended with Southern victory—i. e., with per-

manent independence for the Confederacy. On the contrary, Lincoln made it clear that there could be no suspension of the fighting short of an end to the war, and for this ending he insisted that restoration of the national authority was indispensable.

Thus the conference broke up in deadlock, for which each government blamed the other; but in a further study the meeting has significance as showing some of Lincoln's attitudes. Once the war ended with union and the acceptance of emancipation, Lincoln indicated at Hampton Roads that he would be generous in other matters. He would favor compensation to slaveowners and would act with the "utmost liberality" as to the seizure of Southern property.

Lincoln had never liked confiscation anyhow. He at first planned to veto the severe confiscation bill of July 17, 1862, had prepared an able veto message, and had signed it (which appears now as a presidential mistake) only because its punitive terms had been modified by a joint resolution, because the act specifically recognized the President's pardoning power in the premises, and because the President had this pardoning power in any case. In keeping with Lincoln's mild policy and the

[127]

harmlessness of his Attorney General, Edward Bates, confiscation never had any vigorous executive enforcement. Indeed the war of the sixties is remarkable for measures passed by Congress with great éclat and impressive debate, and then allowed to rest in peace on the statute books. Cleveland's famous phrase, "innocuous desuetude," fits the case.

Just after the fall of Richmond in April 1865 there came another episode in Lincoln's planning for peace with reunion. There is not time to describe his visit to Richmond, nor to note his alleged surprise call at the Pickett home and his purported kissing of the Pickett infant, but attention should be given to consultations in which Lincoln was reported to have consented to the assembling of the Virginia legislature—i. e., the legislature of the Virginia government within the Confederacy. Withdrawal of Virginia troops in the field was necessarily to have been on the agenda of this legislature if it had met; but much more was anticipated in an address to the people of Virginia, dated April 11, approved by General Weitzel of the United States army and signed by an impressive array of Virginia names (see Richmond *Whig*, April 12, 1865). In this address emphasis was placed upon the United States guarantee of safe conduct, transportation, and protection for the legislators and upon the fact that this body would deal with "restoration of peace to the State of Virginia, and the adjustment of questions involving life, liberty and property, that have arisen . . . as a consequence of the war." The complete collapse of Confederate authority and the lack of any agency in the South other than state governments that could handle these adjustments were recognized factors in the existing chaotic situation. Lincoln realized that genuine Southern leaders could and would co-operate to make the situation orderly instead of chaotic, and that their help was essential if this high purpose was to be accomplished quickly and reasonably.

There was a wretched sequel to this Lincoln offer of protection for a reconvened session of the pro-Confederate Virginia legislature. On returning to Washington Lincoln found that he had Stanton, as well as the vindictives generally, to deal with. Dealing with these people was like humoring spoiled children. They demanded attention not by the reasonableness of their attitude but by the fuss and noise of their vociferous outcries. To prevent an explosion at home Lincoln therefore issued a

disclaimer of any intention to consider the "in-
surgent legislature" as the "rightful legislature of
the State." Referring to a misconstruction of his
intention, Lincoln then (April 12) withdrew his
authorization for this session of the Virginia legislature before the session could begin, and the
episode ended in a miserable anticlimax.

So much appears easily on the surface. What is
not so obvious, and what one fails to find sufficiently indicated in Nicolay and Hay, is that Lincoln at Washington had to retreat from the
generosity and practical wisdom of Lincoln at
Richmond; but that, taking all things into con-
sideration, it was the Richmond phase that represented Lincoln's genuine intention. On this point
one should read the account by John A. Campbell,
who had interviews with Lincoln at the time of the
President's visit to Richmond. The Alabama
statesman was favorably impressed by Lincoln's
attitude and believed that the President "felt a
genuine sympathy for the bereavement, destitu-
tion, impoverishment, waste, and overturn that
war had occasioned at the South. . . ." (*Southern
Historical Society Papers,* October 1917, p. 63.)

Campbell, who had remained in Richmond
though others of the Confederate cabinet were in

MALICE TOWARD NONE

By Alexander Gardner, April 10, 1865, four days
before the assassination. In contrast to the vigor of the
Hesler profile shown on another page, this photograph of
Lincoln in his last phase shows 'the deep ravages of war,
but it is notable also for its serenity and gentleness. On
the day this was taken Grant and Lee were talking of
Lincoln at Appomattox, Lee having surrendered on the
ninth of April.

flight, and who was imprisoned after the war, was accused of abusing Lincoln's confidence and misrepresenting his promises, but on a showing of the facts Campbell stands vindicated. Lincoln, he said, desired an end of the ruinous war and considered the Virginia legislature an appropriate instrument for the purpose. Campbell stated distinctly and repeatedly that the suggestion to call the "rebel legislature" of Virginia into session for the broad purpose of restoration came first from Lincoln. The Alabama jurist was asking nothing for himself, but in 1865 he was using, indeed risking, his prestige and statesmanship to restore peace, as in 1861 he had labored to avert war. It was Campbell, not the vindictives, who properly interpreted the President; Lincoln and he were speaking the same language.

The record of what was said (much of it informally) in this 1865 phase bears out Campbell's interpretation as to Lincoln's general attitude toward the South, while the testimony of Gustavus A. Myers, former British consul in Richmond, bears him out as to the episode of calling together the Virginia legislature. Myers was present at the interview between Lincoln and Campbell. The account which one finds utterly unsatisfactory is

[131]

that of Nicolay and Hay, who are not only inadequate (giving almost nothing as to the actual
content of Lincoln's conversations at City Point)
but who offer a false rationalization as to what
Lincoln intended, while heaping undeserved abuse
upon Campbell.

What Lincoln did after he returned to the un-
promising atmosphere of Washington was not
merely to explain his policy so as to avoid misrepresentation, but to alter it. This was a bitter
thing for him to do, since it meant a step in the
wrong direction; but a President in a democracy
must have support. He cannot go it alone. The
main bearing of the episode is the light it throws
upon radical planning, if it could be called that.
The course of anti-Southern reconstruction was
taking shape and Lincoln could not prevent it. It is
a great historical error to suppose that the radicals
succeeded in their maneuvers only after Lincoln's
death. The fact is that they were as determined
and as potent in stopping Lincoln as they were
later, with precisely the same intent, in stopping
Johnson.

Lincoln's part in the ending of the war must be
regarded, not as an incident or event, but as an
integrated sequence or chain of events. Not all the

links in the complex chain can be analyzed, but four
of them may be noted: (1) Lincoln consulting with
top commanders at City Point; (2) Grant two
weeks later in conference with Lee, both on April
9 and April 10; (3) Sherman in North Carolina
seeking to promote civil reconstruction on the most
liberal terms; (4) Johnson in that forlorn place
known as the White House, Washington, D.C.

(1) At City Point on the James River, March
27–28, 1865, President Lincoln conferred in person with Generals Grant and Sherman and with
Admiral Porter. Not all of the discussion was
military. Lincoln thought enough blood had been
shed and hoped another battle could be averted.
He talked with the generals and with Admiral
Porter concerning features of the coming peace.
According to Sherman's account, emphatically
corroborated by Porter, the President wanted to
get Southern men back to their homes, farms, and
shops. What about Confederate leaders—Jefferson Davis for instance? On this point Lincoln said
very truly that he could not speak his mind openly
—other Presidents have felt the same—but that
he would not object if the Confederate leader
could escape "unbeknown to him." Here he tossed
off a story of a man who remembered his temper-

ance pledge when offered a drink, but who would accept brandy poured "unbeknown" into his lemonade. At this City Point conference—on the *River Queen,* the steamer used at Hampton Roads— Lincoln told Sherman he was "all ready for the civil reorganization of affairs at the South as soon as the war was over." He "distinctly authorized" Sherman to assure Governor Vance and the people of North Carolina that when fighting ceased "they would at once be guaranteed all their rights as citizens of a common country; and that to avoid anarchy the State governments then in existence . . . would be recognized by him as the government *de facto* till Congress could provide others."

Admiral Porter took notes at this conference, which Sherman did not do, and the Admiral's account has special interest. He testified that Mr. Lincoln came down to City Point "with the most liberal views" toward the Confederates. He and Grant understood each other perfectly, said Porter; the whole record indicates that Grant's terms to Lee, and Sherman's original terms to Johnston (magnanimously covering the essentials of civil reconstruction), were authorized by Lincoln. It is hard to conceive that these terms would have been offered, put in writing, and duly signed on both sides, if they had not been so authorized. That the Sherman-Johnston convention was later revoked is another story.

(2) What happened at Appomattox is well known. It will not be repeated here, but several points may be singled out for comment. In this terrible year 1945 one stands amazed to note the ease with which the ending of the war was arranged. Lee's aide and secretary, Colonel Charles Marshall, wrote of the meeting of Lee and Grant: "I cannot describe it. I cannot give you any idea of the kindness, and generosity, and magnanimity of those men." It is susceptible of proof that Grant's attitude was Lincoln's attitude also. At City Point the pattern had been set.

This easiest, simplest, and least formal of surrenders occurred on April 9; but another meeting of Lee and Grant occurred on April 10, concerning which too little has been said in the books. It was one of those doubly informal meetings that do not get into state papers. Lee wrote no memoirs and the account in Grant's deathbed memoirs is inadequate. We need not bother about the controversy whether the conversation occurred under an apple tree—the apples were not ripe anyhow—but we are concerned with a most interesting sug-

gestion made by Grant. Colonel Marshall states
what Lee told him when he came back: "General
Lee told me . . . that General Grant asked him
if he would go and meet Mr. Lincoln. He said he
did not know where Mr. Lincoln was . . . but he
said, 'I want you to meet him. Whatever you and
he agree upon will be satisfactory to the reasonable
people of the North and South.' He said: 'If you
and Mr. Lincoln will agree upon terms, your influence in the South will make the Southern people
accept what you accept, and Mr. Lincoln's influence in the North will make reasonable people
of the North accept what he accepts, and all my
[Grant's] influence will be added to Mr. Lincoln's.' " (Maurice, *An Aide-de-Camp of Lee*,
p. 275.)

Lee was a soldier. Jefferson Davis, though in
flight, was still President of the Confederacy, and
Lee could not undertake to "make any terms" of
civil peace. Yet Grant's proposal that Lee should
go to see Lincoln holds great interest; it holds also
that element of poignancy that belongs to all these
thoughts of "reasonable people" in a day when the
most reasonable suggestions were those that were
most frustrated. Years passed, and there came an
unexpected confirmation that such a proposal had

Courtesy of the Illinois State Historical Library

GENERAL LEE ON SOUTHERN
RESTORATION

A page from the diary of Orville H. Browning of Illinois. At White Sulphur Springs in 1868 Browning meets Lee who recalls a conversation with Grant at Appomattox. Lee had referred to Southern readiness for peace. Grant, having seen Lincoln a few days before, was of like mind and urged Lee to see Lincoln, offering safe conduct.

been made. On September 2, 1868, Orville H. Browning of Illinois—Southern-born lawyer, friend of Lincoln, cabinet member under Johnson —wrote of conversing with Lee at White Sulphur Springs. By this account, Lee himself told of Grant's urging him to see Lincoln, for which Grant offered safe conduct. When Lee declined, Grant "still urged it," being "anxious" that the meeting should occur.

Neither at the time nor in historical writing was much attention given to this idea of a conference between the President of the United States and the leading Southern general. It was never more than an offhand suggestion. Some might call it a bit naïve, for if such a meeting had been held were there not senators and congressmen who would have suspected the worst and who might not have remained silent? The matter cannot be dropped, however, without a mental picture of such a conference nor without the reflection that Grant had come fresh from Lincoln when the offer was made.

The convention of surrender at Appomattox, unlike Sherman's intended terms to Johnston, did become a completed fact. It was not overruled, and at least two points concerning this convention between Lee and Grant should be noted. The first

[137]

is that Lincoln's purpose, as shown at City Point, prevailed. The second is that in spite of their brevity and military emphasis, the terms at the McLean house contained one important element bearing upon political reconstruction in the provision that "each officer and man will be allowed to return to their homes not to be disturbed by United States authority so long as they observe their parole and the laws in force where they may reside." (Facsimile in Grant's *Personal Memoirs,* II, 496.) This meant that Confederate soldiers so paroled—which soon came to include all the Confederate armies—could not be prosecuted in Federal courts for participation in the war. Postwar correspondence shows that Grant considered this to be binding upon United States civil authorities, that he took the matter seriously, that he was peculiarly interested in the subject, which involved his pledged word, that he made his views known to an Attorney General who agreed with him, and that in the civil courts former Confederate soldiers and officers were not prosecuted. A few high Confederate civil officials were held briefly in military custody without trial, released, and thereafter unmolested. The "flight into oblivion" concerning which A. J. Hanna has so vividly written, was for the most part unnecessary. Jefferson Davis was not brought to trial, though he was voluminously and tautologically indicted. In his case there was the severity of a long military imprisonment, and Wirz of Andersonville was unfortunately consigned to execution by a military commission that gave too little heed to surrender terms; but these two cases of severity were exceptional. The almost universal policy as to prosecution of individuals who had supported the Lost Cause was nonvindictive, and this nonvindictiveness was largely of Lincoln's doing.

(3) Negotiations between Sherman and Joseph E. Johnston were part of the sequence. Sherman's terms to Johnston under date of April 18, 1865, covered civil reconstruction. They included executive recognition of Southern state governments on taking the Federal oath, with guarantee of political, personal, and property rights, as well as amnesty and freedom from prosecution, to Southern people. Perhaps Sherman exceeded his military authority; but practical solutions were the main thing, and one cannot doubt that the Union general was vastly nearer the true policy than the vindictive Stanton who bluntly repudiated and overruled him. Sherman felt he was acting under "Lincoln's

very eyes," and that his terms were in the spirit of Lincoln's second inaugural. By Admiral Porter's statement, "the terms . . . between . . . [Sherman] and Johnston were exactly in accordance with Mr. Lincoln's wishes." Porter, who as we have seen had been at City Point and had made notes, added that Sherman "could not have done any thing which would have pleased the President better." (Sherman, *Memoirs,* II, 330.) There was sound reason for Alexander H. Stephens's statement that Sherman in his generous terms to Johnston acted in conformity with Lincoln's "uniformly avowed policy," probably indeed "under express authority . . . from Mr. Lincoln himself."

(4) Coming to the fourth point of our sequence, we should note that President Andrew Johnson was accomplishing things on an extensive scale in 1865. All the seceded area was far advanced toward restoration by July 1865, and, except for congressional approval, the process of harmonious and reasonable reconstruction was virtually completed by early December 1865, this being the month in which the antislavery amendment became a part of the Constitution. In this policy Johnson was but pursuing the program of Lincoln. If cita-

tions are needed to establish this continuity, one finds them on diligent search, though the evidence on this point has seldom been adequately presented. Seward stated in 1867 that Johnson's plan "grew during the administration of Mr. Lincoln." (*House Report No. 7*, 40 Cong., 1 sess., 78–79 [first pagination], 401 [second pagination].) Further confirmation is found in postwar letters to Johnson by Ward Lamon and Gideon Welles. (These letters are in the Johnson MSS. in the Library of Congress under dates of Feb. 26, 1866, and July 27, 1869.) Virginia-born Lamon, who knew Lincoln intimately and talked freely with him, wrote that the President intended to "exert all his authority . . . to bring about an immediate and perfect reconciliation between the . . . sections. . . ." Determined to have a vigorous prosecution of the war, wrote Lamon, he was "equally determined upon a 'vigorous prosecution of peace.'" Had Lincoln lived on during the days of reconstruction, it was the view of this intimate friend that the radicals would have been "as loud in their denunciation of his policy as they are of yours [Johnson's]." Thad Stevens's "demand for the head of 'that man at the other end of the Avenue' would not have been a whit less ferocious."

This is corroborated by Gideon Welles, who resented Stanton's vehement opposition to Lincoln's policy and his subsequent perversion of the facts with a view to ruining Johnson. His letter of July 27, 1869, to Johnson, then no longer President, though long and elaborate, should be read in full. Only a brief quotation can be given here. Welles wrote:

After the fall of Richmond and the surrender of Lee, Stanton became alarmed. President Lincoln was for immediate conciliation, harmony and Union. He had, before the surrender of Lee and while at the front, made his mild and conciliatory policy known to Grant and Sherman in interviews which then took place between them. Those interview[s], with their peaceful injunctions, are the key to the easy and magnanimous terms prescribed by Grant to Lee at Appomattox, and by Sherman to Johnston which Stanton, in a way which you know full well, vehemently rebuked and denounced. Genl. Weitzel's proclamation, assembling the rebel legislature at Richmond, was the act of Mr. Lincoln, and Sherman's terms of capitulation were from the same source—

The savage attacks upon Johnson were in reality attacks upon a postwar projection of the martyred Lincoln. It is mere conjecture to say that Lincoln "could have" succeeded against this formidable congressional opposition where Johnson failed. The radicals had deadlocked with Lincoln in 1864. Until they learned more about Johnson there is evidence that the coarser souls among them felt inward satisfaction that the lenient Lincoln had been removed from their path. This meant, however, that they were angry at Lincoln for disagreeing with them rather than that they were willing to allow him actually to obstruct their measures.

Since Johnson was a projection of Lincoln, it is worth noting that in at least three respects (and there were more), Andrew Johnson did not fail. (1) He applied pardon in Lincolnian terms till it became complete on Christmas Day 1868. (2) He used moderate discretion in making appointments that had to do with the postwar South. (3) In the important years from 1865 to 1868, when Congress was offering no solution (not even carpetbaggism), actual home-rule governments were in fact set up by Johnson. The South had to have state governments in these struggling years of the immediate postwar phase. Johnson supplied them. Except as to Tennessee, Congress did not set up its pattern of state governments until 1868. The importance of this development, which might be called a Johnson achievement in Lincolnian terms, will be recognized if one tries to envisage the impossible situation that would have existed in the South if state governments had been kept in suspension until Congress conferred the blessing of radical recognition. In many of the historical accounts the significance of this accomplishment by Johnson has been obscured, largely because of an overemphasis upon formal readmission to the Union with representation in Congress as if that were the sum total of reconstruction. Without underestimating such readmission it must be remembered that state governments at home were a more imperative necessity than representation at Washington.

Such was the sequence: Lincoln and his generals at City Point; Grant in conferences with Lee at Appomattox; Sherman in North Carolina giving Lincolnian terms to Johnston which were later revoked; Andrew Johnson in Washington seeking to carry out the martyred President's program. In this sequence the parts were joined in true continuity, and at every step Lincoln's hand was seen.

Perhaps Lincoln's plan was not sufficiently elaborate. It may have been too forthright and simple. The common man could understand it: pardon for the past, absence of prosecution and persecution, acceptance of emancipation (though some of Lincoln's statements seem to imply concessions here), loyalty for the future, reunion, amnesty for Confederates, return of confiscated property, home rule for the South. The plan excluded ironclad oaths, further confiscations and punishments, carpetbag rule, disfranchisement for supporting the Lost Cause, and a multitude of politician-made abuses that were to come in the period of postwar confusion.

One might ask whether Lincoln's plan had much effect in shortening the war. It can be shown that copies of the President's proclamation of December 8, 1863, were deliberately distributed in a manner calculated to reach soldiers and civilians in the South. It was ordered that in making raids or reconnaissances into the enemy's lines, there should be a special detail of men instructed to spread the proclamation broadcast among soldiers and people in highways and byways. Today such a procedure would be called psychological warfare. Just what was the effect of all this it is hard to say; it appears that peace societies in the South and

[145]

other popular activities designed to shorten the war found their activating forces elsewhere than in Lincoln's announced policy.

To let the matter rest there, however, would be to miss the point. The real answer concerning Southern reaction to Lincoln's program is to be seen in the ease with which Lincoln's conditions were fulfilled under Johnson between April and December 1865. To get the significance of Lincoln's announcements, such as his main speech on reconstruction—the last speech of his life, April 11, 1865—one must note that their appeal was directed more to the Northern than to the Southern mind. In this last speech Lincoln gave no sign of worrying about the South. The real tug for him was to rally his own government, especially Congress. What Lincoln was trying to do, with an earnestness that seems pathetic despite the triumph in the air, was to mold his own people into some unified understanding of peace and restoration. What hurt him was that "loyal people" in the North differed among themselves. It was for this, not for any personal feeling, that he deplored the attacks that he knew to be directed against himself in connection with his plan as applied to Louisiana. It was for this that he did his best in this

last speech of his life to discard immaterial points
and put all the emphasis upon bringing the states
again into their "proper practical relation with the
Union." As with Wilson, Lincoln's greatest task
was at home. The problem was internal unity for
an enlightened postwar regime.

It would challenge the hardiest historian to
analyze those phases of Lincoln and the South that
were related to the party aspect. Where there was
misunderstanding, as of course there was, between
Lincoln and the people of Dixie, much of it arose
from the exigencies and limitations of a party
which, as Avery Craven has said, was in 1860 "a
raw, unformed thing made up of widely divergent
elements held together only by the hostility to
slavery expansion and the desire for office."
("Southern Attitudes toward Abraham Lincoln,"
Papers in Illinois History, 1942, p. 14.) As he
grew in stature Lincoln came to think less highly
of the party motive. In one of his famous wartime
letters (to Erastus Corning and others, June 12,
1863) he wrote: "In this time of national peril I
would have preferred to meet you upon a level
. . . higher than any party platform, because ɪ
am sure that from such more elevated position we
could do better battle for the country we all love

than we possibly can from those lower ones where, from the force of habit, the prejudices of the past, and selfish hopes of the future, we are sure to expend much of our ingenuity and strength in finding fault with and aiming blows at each other." It is true that in this passage Lincoln was chiding certain men of the opposite party because he did not consider them sufficiently nonpartisan, but it is also true that in the same letter he referred with respect to "all those Democrats who are nobly exposing their lives and shedding their blood."

Lincoln appointed Democrats—yes, actually— and they did him good service. If one looks for the complete opposite of Lincoln's policy and program, he finds it not among the Democrats, but among the Jacobins. Men of his own party sought to remove him as candidate in 1864; after the war they seized the party and that was the end of Lincoln's policy of postwar readjustment. Lincoln himself recognized the importance of the opposite party in the promoting of his program. A Democrat named Hogan—"Honest John Hogan," he was called, of southern Illinois and later of St. Louis—wrote a significant letter to President Johnson on June 19, 1865. (Johnson MSS., Library of Congress.) After commenting on the

rising opposition to Lincoln within the Republican
party just before his assassination, and after noting how party associates opposed Lincoln's lenient
policy, Hogan stated that Lincoln had advised him
to remain a Democrat, in order to bring Democratic members into a united front with his own
moderate Republican friends, and thus to maintain
a majority in the Thirty-Ninth Congress (the one
that would begin its session in 1865) "in order to
carry out his conciliatory purposes."

One does not need to belabor the point that the
postwar Republican party was no longer a Lincoln
party. The fact is well known. In this connection it
is instructive to inquire as to the subsequent party
attitude of Lincoln's friends; the answer might
bring some surprises. Part of the story is that
Lincoln had fewer political friends than is often
supposed. John Todd Stuart was a friend, political
mentor, and first partner of the young Lincoln. He
was with Lincoln in the Whig days, but he never
joined the Republican party. In 1860 he supported
Bell. In 1862 he was elected as a Democrat for
Congress, defeating the President's supporter,
Leonard Swett. This occurred in Lincoln's own
congressional district in a wartime election in
which a number of states, including Illinois, that

had supported Lincoln in 1860, sent Democratic delegations to the House of Representatives.

What is more striking, however, than the case of Stuart is that many of Lincoln's Republican associates found reason in postwar times to depart from their Republican affiliations. This was true of Orville H. Browning, who never after 1860 gave active support to a Republican presidential candidate; of Salmon P. Chase, who voiced from the Supreme Court bench his hope that the Liberal Republican ticket would succeed in 1872; of William H. Herndon, Lincoln's law partner over many years, who supported the Liberal Republican ticket in 1872 and who wrote disparagingly of Benjamin Harrison's administration.

There were others in the same category, including men of great prominence. David Davis had been judge of Lincoln's judicial circuit in Illinois, promoter of his nomination in 1860, and upholder of the President's war powers in the *Prize Cases* of 1863, when dissent by one additional member of the Supreme Court would have changed the five-to-four result, placing Lincoln's early war measures as President under the cloud of illegality. Yet Davis opposed radical reconstruction, withheld his vote from Grant in 1868, became a leader against Grant in 1872, and in the Hayes-Tilden controversy commanded enough of the confidence of Democrats to be favored by them as the fifth (and pivotal) Supreme Court member of the electoral commission of 1877. He did not serve on the commission, having become unavailable by being chosen senator from Illinois. Thus negatively he may have helped Hayes (at least so people thought), but in later years as United States senator he held aloof from the Republicans, attending the caucus of no party.

Only a few other instances can be mentioned. Leonard Swett, who as congressional candidate bore Lincoln's standard to defeat in 1862, departed from the Republican fold in 1872. Lyman Trumbull, Republican senator from Illinois during Lincoln's administration, left the main Republican track to vote for Johnson's acquittal in 1868 and to oppose Grant in 1872. In that same year the anti-Grant Liberals counted in their ranks Jesse W. Fell of Bloomington, Illinois, who had been one of the earliest men to promote Lincoln as presidential timber and had been his stanch supporter in 1860.

John M. Palmer of Illinois was a Republican in Lincoln's day. He played his part in the early beginnings of the party in the state. Yet after the war disgust with the Grant administration drove him first into the Liberal Republican party and later into the Democratic party. Having been elected Republican governor of Illinois in 1868, his party shift carried him to the point where he was defeated as candidate for governor on the Democratic side in 1888 and elected Democratic senator in 1891. He was a Cleveland Democrat and headed the hopeless Palmer-Buckner ticket in 1896. It will not do to dismiss Palmer as a turncoat. There was more genuine significance in his politics than in that of party regulars.

Gideon Welles was so opposed to Grant and the radicals in 1868 that, according to his diary of July 14 of that year, he had "no alternative but to go for Seymour." Montgomery Blair in 1865 publicly explained that he was leaving the Republican party. He supported Seymour in 1868, Greeley in 1872, and Tilden in 1876, even serving as Tilden's counsel before the electoral commission. In 1877 Blair said: "I have been on the Democratic side in every political contest . . . since 1865. . . ." (Blair MSS., Library of Congress, Nov. 22, 1877.) James Speed, Attorney General under Lincoln, favored Grover Cleveland in 1884. Ward Lamon, Lincoln's intimate friend and almost his bodyguard, strongly disliked the radical wing of the Republican party, formed a partnership with the Democrat, Jeremiah S. Black, and chose Black's son, Chauncey F., as ghost writer of the Lamon biography of Lincoln. Gustav Koerner, Illinois Republican, joined the seceding Liberals in 1872.

Three outstanding editors of Lincoln's day were Horace Greeley, Charles A. Dana, and Henry J. Raymond. Greeley was a Republican; certainly the other two vigorously supported Lincoln. After the war Greeley broke with Grant, becoming the Liberal Republican and Democratic candidate for the presidency in 1872. Dana made his *Sun* a Democratic paper, severely attacked the Grant administration, and referred to Hayes as a receiver of stolen goods. Raymond died in June 1869, too soon to reveal his attitude toward the Grant administration, but he had so far broken with the Republican policy of reconstruction as to participate prominently in the Philadelphia convention of 1866 whose specific purpose was to promote the election of congressmen who would support Johnson's generous policy.

These matters are not brought into the discussion for any partisan motive. One may well judge that Johnson, Browning, Davis, Trumbull, Mont-

[153]

gomery Blair, Raymond, and their colleagues re-
flected Lincoln more truly in policy and personality
than the "politicos" or stalwarts of the dominant
party in postwar decades, but the conclusion to be
drawn from it all is that memories of Lincoln had
better not be preserved in partisan terms. What
Lincoln himself would have done in party affiliation
if he had lived for two or three decades after the
war can only be a matter of conjecture. The solid
thing we do know is his support of magnanimous
reconstruction and of liberal principles during his
lifetime. We know further that Lincoln was least
partisan in those aspects in which he was greatest.

Any account of Lincoln and the South would be
incomplete if it did not include some of the tributes
of Southerners after his death. In a Virginia family
which the present speaker knows well (having married into it) there is a tradition which can be
matched at many a Dixie fireside. When the news
of Lincoln's assassination came to southwestern
Virginia the head of this family, a minister, said
with bowed head: "The South has lost its best
friend." A search of Southern newspaper comments at the time of Lincoln's assassination would
be of real interest. For our purpose it may suffice
to give one example. With mourning bands on its

editorial page the Richmond (Virginia) *Whig* on the Monday after Lincoln's death (April 17) spoke as follows:

The heaviest blow which has ever fallen upon the people of the South has descended. Abraham Lincoln, the President of the United States, has been assassinated! . . . [T]he time, manner, and circumstances of President Lincoln's death render it the most momentous, the most appalling, the most deplorable calamity which has ever befallen the people of the United States. . . . Just as everything was happily conspiring to a restoration of tranquility, under the benignant and magnanimous policy of Mr. Lincoln, comes this terrible blow. God grant that it may not rekindle excitement or inflame passion again.

One might ask: Was the *Whig* editor expressing his genuine sentiment, or should one attribute this favorable appraisal of Lincoln to the fact that Richmond was then under Federal military control? If one consults *Virginia Newspapers, 1821–1935,* by Lester J. Cappon (pp. 24, 192), he finds that on the fall of Richmond there was a very brief suspension of the *Whig,* after which the paper was published "with the consent of the military authorities" and with the following announcement: "the *Whig* will . . . be issued hereafter as a

Union paper. The sentiments of attachment to our
'whole country,' which formerly characterized it as
a journal, will again find expression in its columns."
To this end "Robert Ridgway, whose connections
with the paper had been severed in 1861 because of
his pro-unionism, again became editor. . . ." A
strict interpretation of the words just quoted would
indicate that the main break in the continuity of
Whig doctrine was from 1861 to 1865. After the
war the paper was subject to possible suspension,
but the whole background of this editor, a genuine
Southerner, indicates that his true opinion was expressed in the editorial of April 17. The question
is not whether Richmond was under Federal control—that is known—but whether Ridgway was
sincere. He was a man not of servile but of fear-
less character; he expressed views of which Northern radicals disapproved, as in July of 1865. His
statements may be set alongside numerous Southern comments. On the tragedy of Lincoln's death
and the magnanimity of his policy his words have
the substance and tone of sincerity.

It would be equally significant to note the com-
ments of military leaders in the South. Robert E.
Lee, who considered Lincoln's call for troops in
April 1861 unconstitutional, showed no continuing

Assassination of President Lincoln!

The heaviest blow which has ever fallen upon the people of the South has descended. Abraham Lincoln, the President of the United States, has been assassinated! The decease of the Chief Magistrate of the nation, at any period, is an event which profoundly affects the public mind, but the time, manner, and circumstances of President Lincoln's death render it the most momentous, the most appalling, the most deplorable calamity which has ever befallen the people of the United States.

The thoughtless and the vicious may affect to derive satisfaction from the sudden and tragic close of the President's career, but every reflecting person will deplore the awful event. Just as everything was happily conspiring to a restoration of tranquility, under the benignant and magnanimous policy of Mr. Lincoln, comes this terrible blow. God grant that it may not rekindle excitement or inflame passion again.

That a state of war, almost fratricidal, should give rise to bitter feelings and bloody deeds in the field was to be expected, but that the assassin's knife and bullet should follow the great and best loved of the nation in their daily walks and reach them when surrounded by their friends, is an atrocity which will shock and appall every honorable man and woman in the land.

The secrecy with which the assassin or assassins pursued their victim indicates that there were but few accomplices in this inhuman crime. The abhorrence with which it is regarded on all sides, will, it is hoped, deter insane and malignant men from the emulation of the infamy which attaches to this infernal deed.

We cannot pursue the subject further. We contemplate too deeply and painfully the terrible aspects of this calamity to comment upon it further.

The facts, as we have officially ascertained them, are subjoined: The President visited Ford's Theatre Friday night, and about thirty minutes past ten...

In the early months of the government, Southern leaders proclaimed that slavery was an element of military strength to the South; that the slaves would work the farms, raise corn, wheat and bacon, while the white men fought in the armies. For some time this delusion continued. But in proportion as the advance of the United States armies occurred, the inevitable result, foreseen by the wiser of Southern statesmen, followed. The solution of the question of slavery has been purely the result of the laws of war. When the South invited war, she abandoned slavery. To suppose that invading enemies would fail to weaken their adversaries by calling to their aid such of the male population of the invaded country as would join them, was a delusion which only madness could have cherished.

The Southern slave owners have discovered by the revelations of the war that, however faithful and personally attached to them their negroes may have been, they desire freedom. They must now admit that slavery has received its death blow. The last and most fatal wound was inflicted by the South herself. When slaves were invited to volunteer for military service, the tacit admission was made that they were persons privileged to enter into the military elements of the struggle between the North and the South, and that, therefore, the military measures and policy which freed them were legitimate results of the state of war.

The change which has thus been effected is of momentous import. To change the status of the whole laboring class of a country as wide as the Southern States is a work which cannot go on without extensive embarrassment and dislocation. To substitute for the involuntary servitude formerly prevailing the voluntary servitude in which contracts are made, wages are allowed, time is computed and all the relations of the free labor system are recognized, will require time and patience. But the work has been commenced, and the wise among our people will soon be satisfied that their condition will not be the worse for the change. The emancipated negroes will also learn that if they will eat they must work, and that industry and good temper are their best policy.

AMERICAN VESSELS FIRED UPON BY A PORTUGUESE FORT.

The United States frigates Niagara and Sacramento have for some time been engaged in chasing the rebel ram Stonewall. The latter has at length succeeded in escaping from the port of Ferrol. On March 27th her arrival in Lisbon, the capital of Portugal, is announced. The Portuguese authorities ordered her to leave the harbor. The Niag...

SOUTHERN MOURNING FOR THE FALLEN LINCOLN

Lincoln's visit to Richmond was fresh in mind. On April 12, the Richmond *Whig* had printed an appeal of leading Virginians urging co-operation by the legislature in the task of peace. Not bitterness, but a lofty spirit of conciliation had been expressed by the *Whig* prior to Lincoln's death.

hard feeling toward him in the postwar days. More than twenty years after Lincoln's death General Beauregard wrote to a gentleman in Springfield, Illinois, who had invited him to attend a memorial ceremony for the martyred President. In thought only, said the Southern general, could he pay homage to the memory of a great and a good man. He wrote of Lincoln's "unalloyed ambition" and "purity of purpose." At the time of his "untimely taking off" his life was "invaluable," wrote Beauregard; he was "of extraordinary importance to the country he served so well." (Dated at New Orleans, April 5, 1889, the original letter is in the Illinois State Historical Library.)

In 1880 Mr. O. H. Oldroyd sent out appeals far and wide for comments on Lincoln; he assembled them in an unsatisfactory book called *The Lincoln Memorial: Album Immortelles.* Among the contributors were John Bright (whose indirect relation to Lincoln had been that of truest friendship and real understanding), Cassius M. Clay, Charles A. Dana, Thomas A. Edison, U. S. Grant, David D. Porter, Asa Gray, Parke Godwin, Oliver Wendell Holmes (the doctor-poet), William H. Herndon, Benson J. Lossing, Henry W. Longfellow, Joshua F. Speed, J. G. Whittier, and Charles W.

Warner. It is not, however, the *Album Immortelles*
itself that interests us, so much as the autograph
letters of which the original manuscripts are to be
found in the collection of Mr. Oliver R. Barrett of
Chicago.

Along with men of differing views, a number of
Southerners contributed to this collection. C. F.
Burnam, attorney at Richmond, wrote of Lincoln
as having "first place" among men of the century.
M. F. Bigney, writing from the "Daily City Item,
39 Natchez Street, New Orleans" (this letterhead
being omitted in the book), showed a deep feeling
that burst into poetry; he referred to Lincoln's
death as "a dire calamity" to the South. The illus-
trious historian of Louisiana, Charles Gayarré, in
a longer letter than Oldroyd printed, wrote of
Lincoln as "one . . . whose sad end was univer-
sally deplored." Lincoln, he said, was "humane
and pure, kindly disposed toward the South." His
"tragic death," he added, "was a most fatal event
for the Southern States."

One could go on quoting Southerners in this collection, but one more must suffice. Alexander H.
Stephens, writing at Washington on January 18,
1882, referred to Lincoln as a Whig associate in
the old days, gave interesting descriptive touches,
recalled Lincoln's readiness with anecdote, and

confessed "a high . . . personal regard" for the man, despite political differences. Lincoln's nature, said Stephens, "overflowed with . . . human kindness." In this Oldroyd letter Stephens called attention to his estimate of Lincoln in a speech before the House of Representatives in Washington, February 12, 1878, on the occasion of presenting the Carpenter painting of the emancipation proclamation. It was one of those steps on the "road to reunion" in which hatreds were forgotten. An analogous occasion was L. Q. C. Lamar's eulogy of Sumner, April 27, 1874.

The blight that spread over the South after Lincoln was not without its effect upon the whole country. After eight decades one still sees its consequences. If the road to reunion was not blocked, it was diverted by ugly detours and it stopped short of its proper destination. In the case of both Lincoln and Wilson the soldiers did their part and so did the Executive, but in each case partisanship and narrow-mindedness wrecked the program. Under Lincoln and Johnson, as under Wilson, there was failure of high-minded unity behind the plan of peace that bore promise of success. In each case, instead of needful co-operation, there was stupid deadlock between President and Congress. There was in each case a fateful congressional election whose effect was felt far down in later years: 1918 may be matched against the "critical year" 1866. In each case the President's plan failed in the sense that it failed to be adopted; the opposite plan in each case failed miserably by being adopted.

It was a reactionary or negative choice that was made in the rejection of Lincoln's as of Wilson's plan. In each episode the rejection was bound up with a whole complex of reactionary attitudes. In each instance the negative plan broke down in practice. Reconstruction after Lincoln failed. So also did isolationism after Wilson. In the one case as in the other the President's opponents shook their manes with lofty unction, yet at other times they used the language of alleged realism, as did Chamberlain; but who would now say that Thaddeus Stevens or Chandler, or Ben Wade, or Hiram Johnson, Borah or Lodge, were either knights in shining armor or realists who knew all the answers?

Once more far-reaching problems of peace are upon us, and the unhappy periods after 1865 and after 1918 should be restudied for the unmistakable lessons they carry.

To remember Lincoln is to remember his ideals.

Sometimes we tend to dismiss a leader's ideals too cavalierly. Or sometimes we pin the wrong labels on people and call the wrong ones "realists." It has not been in pursuing ideals that this nation has gone wrong. It has been in following the lead, or the drift, of negative men that we have fallen into disaster. We do not have to be perfectionists either. It has been said that ideals are like stars: we do not reach them, but we do steer by them. The study of history will be of some use if it enables us to remember that our true leaders are not the obstructionists, nor those who negatively exploit every disagreement or difficulty. Leaders in a challenging emergency should not set their sights too low. They will do well to remember with Herbert Agar that there is "a time for greatness." Rightly considered, history is no merely academic subject. Historical insight can become the truest foresight. On the broader world stage which the present era demands it is well to recapture the significance of Woodrow Wilson's "organized opinion of mankind" and of Abraham Lincoln's "just and lasting peace among ourselves and with all nations."